WITHDRAWN

Profiles

PROFILES

*People Who Are Helping to
Change the World*

HELEN KOOIMAN HOSIER

HAWTHORN BOOKS, INC.
Publishers/NEW YORK

Contents

Introduction

I have always been interested in biography. Even as a child I could lose myself in reading about "for real" people; later, moving into adult years, I read everything I could get my hands on that showed me what God was doing through contemporary Christians. The trouble was, however, that I couldn't find enough of such reading material. I knew God was at work in the world, and thus perhaps it's not too surprising that, after I started writing, I decided that these stories of what God was doing through ordinary but deeply dedicated people should be written and kept for posterity. Was the Holy Spirit whispering in my ear telling me something that I should do? I listened carefully. The idea persisted.

In 1968 my first biographical account of some of God's precious jewels came into being in the form of *Cameos: Women Fashioned by God.* That volume is numbered among the best-selling Christian books worldwide.

"You need to do a companion book to *Cameos,*" I was told by more than one individual.

"God," I prayed, "are you trying to tell me something?" He was! And in 1972 *Silhouettes: Women Behind Great Men* was published.

Readers asked for more. Others we discovered also liked biography and reading about contemporary Christians.

I'm grateful to you, the reader, for your interest and keen discernment. Your letters and comments through the years have been a tremendous source of encouragement and motivation to me. I want to acknowledge my gratitude to you.

In both *Cameos* and *Silhouettes* we saw the Holy Spirit moving powerfully in the lives of yielded individuals. Now once again it has been my privilege to draw together this third in the series of stories demonstrating the continuing work of the Holy Spirit through men and women who are working to help change the world for Christ. The impact of these people and their God-given and God-blessed work is more far reaching than anyone can visualize; and yet I found each person to be so transparently open and honest, so beautifully down to earth and ordinary, that I felt I'd known them all my life. Perhaps this in itself gives us a clue as to why God should choose to entrust them with their particular gift, and in this, too, we can learn something.

I am certain that, given the opportunity, you, the reader, would join me in thanking these individuals for sharing their experiences in these *Profiles.*

The book is sent forth gratefully with the prayer that God will use it to inspire and motivate others to make the most of their God-given talents and allow the Holy Spirit to develop these gifts into great usefulness and effectiveness for Christ as you also help to change the world.

Profiles

Charlie and Harriet Barrows

1

No Rocking Chair, Please!

AGRICULTURIST
CHARLES BARROWS

At 5:13 A.M. on April 18, 1906, San Francisco, California, was rocked by a heavy earthquake. In three days earthquake, fire, and dynamite had killed 700 persons and destroyed 497 blocks of buildings covering four-and-a-half square miles. It was a holocaust that left indelible impressions upon the Bay area's survivors. In nearby Berkeley, a small boy clung to his mother. His father was in the city, and mother and son were afraid. "It is the first momentous thing I remember from out of my childhood," says Charles Barrows. God was shifting the contours of the earth.

Some sixty-four years later Barrows was to write a letter from Cebu City in the Philippines to dear ones in the States. He said, "I have been busy spending time changing the face of the earth." In a real physical way he had been doing that very thing—terracing hills, building roads and fire trails, clearing land for agriculture use, and making athletic fields for schools. But in a far more important way, Charles Barrows had been investing his time and energies sharing his love and knowledge of God and the Bible. His involvement with people left an "earthquake" effect upon individuals wherever he went, only in a remarkable way, a good way,

3

that transformed not only the very face of the earth but, more importantly, the lives of those walking upon Philippine soil.

Everyone ends up calling him Charlie. And no wonder! You can't be around Charles Barrows for long without some of that irresistible Charlie charisma rubbing off.

Charlie's character traits showed early in life. The family moved from the Bay area to Ceres, a little town midway between Turlock and Modesto, California, when young Charles was in the second grade. His father became a farmer. "We went to school in a one-room schoolhouse. We rode saddle horses and in hot weather pulled off our clothes and swam with our horses in the canal. We stole cherries, strawberries, pumpkins and watermelons. I was the oldest of three sisters and one brother," he likes to reminisce. "And oh! the escapades I got into!"

The twinkle in his eye indicated that Charlie's memory was serving him well. When he said, "I was always involved in something," I knew he was leaving volumes untold. It wasn't too difficult to visualize Charlie and his cohorts confiscating the cooking-class food from out of the school dumbwaiter, or blowing the windows out of the chemistry room with gunpowder one noon hour! Obviously Charlie has always been a ball of energy, constantly on the move, never content to just coast along.

In another book, *Silhouettes: Women Behind Great Men*, I show how very often behind a great man there is a great woman. Harriet Barrows qualifies.

Charlie and Harriet lived through the Roaring Twenties. One night when Charlie and his best friend were driving around in a Model T Ford, Charlie's friend said, "Are you happy with the girls you've been dating?"

Charlie replied, "No, I'm not. I sure wouldn't want to marry any of them."

His buddy, with a worried tone, said, "Well, what are we going to do about it? One of these days we'll want to get a wife and settle down."

The conversation continued with Charlie questioning, "Well, what do you suggest?"

"How about my cousin Harriet Griggs for you? I'll try to take out the Applegarth girl."

That was the beginning of a courtship that Charlie says cost him many boxes of chocolates, bouquets of flowers, and piano lessons. Piano lessons? Charlie taking piano lessons? "Yes, Harriet's mother was a piano teacher, and I was determined to make headway with Harriet and her mother. Not only was I trying to win Harriet's hand, but her mother needed a lot of coaxing before I won her approval. You see, I wasn't a Christian. Our family didn't go to church except on Christmas and sometimes to 'friendlies' on Wednesday nights. But that was just for the social time.

"I was just about ready to give up when one Sunday morning I told my mother, 'I'm going to church,' and I did—to the church Harriet attended. Harriet sang in the choir, and she about fell out of her seat when she saw me. I sat in the back corner, but as the minister, Rev. Marian McCart, preached, the Lord spoke to my heart. Christ was standing at the door of my heart, but I was on the wrong side of the door. It was an awfully long walk all the way down to the front of that church, but I said yes to Christ.

"Even after that it was tough sledding with Harriet and her mother, but I never gave up."

The Barrows determination won out, and Charlie and Harriet were married shortly after the end of World War I.

Mention Black Bart, Three-fingered Jack, train robberies, Indian trails, and golden poppies to Charlie Barrows, and he says, "Yep, I've lived through those days. Never will forget when they robbed the train outside of Turlock, took the gold out of the safe, and got away on horseback.

"Used to take us two days by horse and buggy to get from Turlock to Sacramento."

Charlie and Harriet have gone from the horse-and-buggy age to the jet era in their lifetimes. "This is one reason I could adapt so well to a civilization that is fifty years behind ours," he says as he tries to hurry our conversation along. He wants to tell me about the Philippines and how God transported them there after retirement from the Turlock area.

"No rocking chair retirement for us," he says, and you know exactly what he means. Charlie in a rocking chair is about as preposterous as a pig trying to smell like a rose. "It sure is an exciting time to live," he continues. "But life at best is so short here on this earth. We need to invest our few days wisely, and seek in every way to use our talents in the lives of others. The Bible teaches that he who would save his life must lose it, and this makes life so very worthwhile."

After marriage Charlie took his bride to the farm. Two years later they tried city life but farming was in Charlie's blood—so it was back to Ceres and the farm. Forty years later they were still on the farm, but in the interim five children were born into their family. Mention the name Barrows most anyplace in the world today and immediately the hearer will think of Cliff Barrows, renowned song leader for the Billy Graham Evangelistic Association. This is Charlie and Harriet's son. But mention the name Barrows in the Philippines and other islands, and people will say, "Charlie Barrows and his wife, Harriet, they did so much for us here. We miss them. We wish they could come back."

That "so much" includes, among other things, distribution of well over a million copies of the Gideon Bible in four years' time. Charles Barrows is the much-respected past president of the Gideons of California/Nevada, and a member of Gideons International for over forty years.

But what brought Charlie and Harriet to the Philippines at a time in their lives when, by almost anyone's standard, they should have decided to leave their California farm home and retire?

Charlie answered that question in a letter to their children written from the Philippines after they reached that destination upon "retirement."

"There comes a time in the experience of nearly every family when all the children have left home and some thought has to be given as to what the parents should do with the old home. It is true that for some families such as ours the home holds a lifetime of memories, and hard work, for much of ourselves has gone into its building.

"But you must decide whether to sit and dream in an empty shell and try to live in the memories that haunt every room (even ink spilled on a new carpet), or to move out and let the years that remain of your life become a new and exciting adventure."

Charlie and Harriet made the latter choice.

Fifty years had been spent in one way or another in the field of agriculture. The name Barrows in California was a symbol of experience in farming and irrigation, as well as in quality control work for three canneries. "My father lived and worked close to the soil all his life," Cliff says. "When it came time for retirement he and mother prayed that God would give them an opportunity to serve him in some capacity that they hadn't yet been privileged to serve in. God laid the Philippines upon their hearts."

How marvelously the Lord works things out! And God must have a sense of humor. He would have to, for he used a silver teapot to enable Charlie Barrows to share his knowledge of farming and to witness for Christ to the president of the Philippines.

When Charlie speaks of it today you sense his awe of the way it all came about.

"As you travel through life, and the years pass by, you suddenly wake up to realize that possibly the years that remain can be counted on your fingers, and then when they are spent, what excuse will you have when you are called before your Savior to give an accounting for a lifetime of living?

"You know that life is something like a book. When you come to the end of a chapter you have two choices; you can go back and reread the chapter you have just finished or turn the page and see what exciting things are ahead. I have found that it is a lot more interesting to turn the page.

"But no new page faced my wife and me as we were confronted with retirement. . . . As we prayed, God opened a door. I know now he showed us where we were needed. Along with the open door, as we prayed, God also delivered us from this captivity to things, which we thought were so necessary for security. We moved out of our home, leaving nearly everything behind us, and made preparations for what I believe we can both honestly say was the most exciting adventure of our lives.

"To prepare our hearts for the challenge before us, God allowed me to make a trip to the Orient in 1966 when missionary Dick Hillis asked me to come over and see how a layman could fit into Christian work there. While I was in the Philippines God spoke to my heart and said, 'This is where I need you. Here you will not have to spend two or more years in language study, but you can get right to work.'

"Long years before, my father had been in the Philippines, and when he returned home he brought back a silver teapot from the home of Philippine President Aquinaldo as a souvenir from the Spanish-American war.

"Now, knowing that I would be going to the Philippines on this trip, I got out the dusty teapot and we shined it up. I told Harriet, 'Maybe I'll be able to get in to see President Marcos with this!' When I called his office, arrangements were made for him to see me and my teapot. When I got there, he accepted not only the teapot but a Gideon Bible.

"When President Marcos learned that I had spent my entire life working in many phases of agriculture in addition to being a buyer and quality control man for big canneries, and that I knew and understood practical farming, he asked, 'Have you ever given any thought to coming over here to help us? We can't offer you money, but we can offer you plenty of opportunity to help and show us things we need to know.'

"I knew there were tremendous needs in the Philippines. In the seventeen days that I was there I spoke twenty-seven times in schools, churches, and service organizations. I looked at their system of farming and their agricultural needs and recognized ways in which I could be of help.

"I came back home, and Harriet and I talked it over and prayed about it. We feel that we moved there under orders from God himself so that we could make those immediate years following retirement really count for Jesus Christ.

"I retired in February 1967. It was three weeks later that we boarded a plane for the Philippines. We had been asked by the president to stay for two years, but we ended up staying five years and three months. I had told Harriet, 'If I once get settled in a rocking chair, it will be hard to get back up, but Harriet, I'm not built for a rocking chair retirement!' " And indeed, he wasn't—but neither was Harriet.

"When we got off the plane in Manila, we had no mission board behind us, so we were free to work as God laid out the plans each day, and we didn't quite know what we were going to do. Mainly, however, we wanted to serve the Lord; we felt this would be a good way to distribute Gideon Bibles. We had no special authority from anybody. It was quite an experience at our ages. We were quite literally in a strange land, and we didn't even know where we were going to stay!

"As we left the airport in Manila, Harriet asked me what we should call our mission. I replied that we were on a mission of helps. That was what we were in the Philippines for— to help wherever we were needed, from repairing machinery to overhauling pumps and working on wells. I even had to design some equipment to help to solve some of our problems.

"I had started with the Gideons thirty years earlier in the real Depression days and was responsible then for raising funds in the churches for the distribution of Bibles in our area.

"That made me eligible to become a Gideon (you have to qualify both spiritually and occupationally—you must have experience in management and have had people working under you)."

That was just the beginning of Charlie's involvement with Gideons International. In succeeding years he was to travel all over the world representing the organization. But now Charlie and Harriet found themselves in the islands of the Philippines.

As Charlie and Harriet stood on Philippine soil in the airport of Cebu City, he remembered the words of President Marcos: "I know very little about agriculture, Mr. Barrows, and yet it is the backbone of our country. We need help. Would you come out and help and be accountable to me?"

In his briefcase Charlie carried a letter bearing the official seal of the Republic of the Philippines requesting, among other things, that the usual courtesies and cooperation be accorded him to make his stay fruitful and at the same time pleasant. His presence was to prove so welcome and of such tremendous help that he was given the status of special agricultural advisor to the republic and a visa that was the equivalent to that granted to embassy personnel. It was an open door that gave him the freedom he needed to visit all the little villages as well as the cities throughout the republic.

As he speaks, Charlie likes to use an illustration that has practical meaning to him. He holds up his Bible and says, "It is like a passport and a visa. You have to have a passport to leave our country, but if you don't have a visa to get into another country you are stuck. The Bible is the only book in the world that contains both a passport and a visa."

After one month in the Philippines Charlie wrote the first of many letters which he refers to as his "epistles from the Philippines."

A few months later Charlie wrote, "To try to sum up the

opportunities and challenge of the Philippines would require that a book be written, and for that I do not have the time. "Little did I realize when I came here how much responsibility I would have. Basically the agriculture problems are much the same as in the States, but the solutions are much more complicated because of local conditions and lack of equipment and supplies."

Charlie saw the need for mechanization to increase production and make available more food for the people. He saw people harvesting the rice by hand with little grass sickles and knew that time was being lost in the harvesting, thereby making impossible the planting of another crop. He was frustrated by the lack of knowledge among the people, many of whom could not read. There were pest-control problems and irrigation needs. He was staggered by the immensity of all the varied urgent needs, both material and spiritual, and more than once wrote, "When we look ahead the responsibilities we face almost overwhelm us."

But their determination and their God-given faith and strength always won out. "To try and share with you all that has happened would be almost impossible, for a wide and effectual door has been opened unto us in so many areas."

Charlie's letters sounded like those from the Apostle Paul written to the Corinthian Christians from Ephesus: "For a great door and effectual is opened unto me, and there are many adversaries" (I Cor. 16:9).

"Surely this is God's time for us to be here," he said. "There is a hunger for God's word that we do not see in the States.

"Each day brings new challenges and new open doors. Pray for us that although we may get weary in the way that we might not be weary of the way, but might set the pace for others out here. It is so easy to get into a rut and so very hard to climb out. It is so easy to get to feeling sorry for yourself and to just give up and quit.

"We do get lonesome for friends and loved ones, but we

are constantly reminded that he who puts his hand to the plow and looks back is not fit for the Kingdom of God. I have come across a phrase that the Chinese use out here. It is 'gung ho,' which simply means working together. I believe that this would be a good motto for every family and church. This sometimes is the hardest lesson that we have to learn."

There was a gentle but an underlying tone of firm insistence in Charlie's letters as he wrote: "For Christian laymen and laywomen there are wide open doors. There are too few of us to get everything done that needs to be accomplished out here. And to think that this is only one needy area of the world.

"I never realized how busy you can be and still be retired!" he inserted with the Barrows humor shining through.

"So many older people, and I guess we qualify in this category, are lonesome and frustrated because they feel they are not needed. If this is your problem you should seek out a mission field, for here God can use whatever talent you may have.

"We have found that the best way to get people to respond to and understand the love of God is in the help we give to them as we witness. It is very difficult to talk about love so others can understand, but when we share our time and our talents with them, they invariably ask us, 'Why do you do this?'

"When we explain to them that because God loves us we want to share our love with them in helping to work out their problems, they will listen and try to understand.

"As I read in the New Testament, and study the life of Jesus, I realize that his ministry was a ministry of helps, that those to whom he ministered might understand God's love. Many times we get impatient and try to push too hard to accomplish the things we desire to complete. I have had to learn to adjust to a society where the level of comprehension is slower than we find in the States. Again, as I look at the life of my Lord, I am made to realize that he was never too busy to take time out to listen and help. I want to be like Jesus.

"We are building no churches, and we are not underwritten by anyone, but we are simply trying to introduce people to the one who is the Way, the Truth, and the Life."

Yes, it was gung ho all the way for Charlie and Harriet.

As he revealed to me his recollections of those years, he said: "We concentrated our first agricultural work in Cebu City (population 600,000 at the time) at the well-known Good Shepherd Orphanage. We terraced the hills and planted 3,000 banana plants. We built a dam across a little creek to provide water for irrigation.

"We won the hearts of the Sisters. The 160 girls there called us uncle and mom. We gained a whole new family, and took five of them at a time for holidays, to substitute for our own children back home. Every time we proved our love and showed that we were there to help them, they wanted to know why, and then we shared the Gospel.

"One day the seventy-eight-year-old Mother Superior asked me to show a Billy Graham film, *The Restless Ones*, which might help some of the graduating class. I went, taking five women for counselors. When an invitation to receive Christ was given, over fifty girls responded. The Mother Superior said, 'The Holy Spirit was speaking today. I could feel him in my heart.' "

That was just the beginning. Door after door began to open in school after school. Then the civic organizations began pleading with Charlie to come and speak. "We forgot denominational barriers over there," he explained, "and simply presented Christ and the need for a loving relationship with him." Hundreds of thousands of Gideon Bibles and Testaments were needed. The call went out, and the Gideons in the States responded.

"The orphanage work opened the door to San Carlos University, the oldest, most important university in the islands.

"We started with the 1,200 Testaments we had and rushed an order to Gideon headquarters. When the shipment came, we gave 14,500 students Testaments, and 1,000 teachers Bibles. The white-haired business manager cried as he said, 'This is the happiest day of my life. For thirty years I've prayed that we might have Bibles in this school.

"Other colleges said, 'If San Carlos needs Bibles, we need them, too.' God let us start at the top! Then we began working down through other colleges and high schools—90 percent of them were Catholic. The doors were open wide!"

In speaking now in the States, Charlie will ask, "Have you ever received a love letter? The Bible is God's love letter to us. A love letter is a very personal thing. We read our love letters over and over again so as not to miss anything. This is what we should do with God's Word."

Charlie and Harriet were giving out God's love letter by the thousands, and their hearts overflowed with joy. "I have been in schools and colleges in the Philippines where I was handing out Bibles and have run out of them. Do you know what it is like to see 1,200 students with outstretched hands begging for Bibles and not to have any left to give them?" he asks with a catch in his voice.

"I always made it a practice, however, not to give out the Word of God without also having an opportunity first to go into the classroom or assembly hall and speak to the students and teachers explaining what the Bible is about.

"In Holy Name High School, the principal went with me from class to class. He reminded the students that for over a year they had been praying for Bibles and that this was the day that God had answered their prayers. It was a wonderful thing to be a tool in the hand of God, used by him to answer prayer in this way," Charlie adds.

I asked Charlie if he had ever had any experiences in which his life was endangered. The effervescent Charlie smiled, scratched his crewcut, and stretched out. "Well, yes," he answered, and then he launched into an account that left me breathless as I hung onto every word.

"If you have ever been in a storm on the ocean, with waves running over six feet high, in a little native boat about twenty-eight feet long and five feet wide and about thirty inches deep, two hours from land with nothing in sight but water, facing heavy winds and a driving rain, you will be thankful that you are a Christian, and that the Bible teaches that all things work together for good when we are in God's care.

"This was the situation that Gideon Clair Layman and I found ourselves in when we endeavored to reach Bantayan Island in March 1971, to distribute New Testaments and Bibles to 2,400 students and teachers in the four high schools on the island. Bantayan Island lies north of the island of Cebu, about one-and-a-half hours by launch, when the launches are running. That day, because of the high wind, the launches were not on schedule, and, as we had sent word that we would be there to distribute Scriptures, we rented a boat to try and keep our appointment on the island. The man who owned the boat was confident that we could make the trip safely.

"The New Testaments and Bibles were in twenty-five cartons, placed on deck amidship and covered with a piece of oilcloth and we were seated on top of the stack to try and keep the oilcloth in place and keep the Scriptures dry. The outriggers, placed on each side of the boat to keep it upright, were all that kept us from overturning as we rode the waves. One of the crew rode the outrigger on the windward side to take the strain off the opposite outrigger when it was under the water. Two of the crew bailed as fast as possible in order to keep the boat from filling with water, and to keep the little nine-horsepower inboard motor dry. At one time the deck was at such a steep angle that both of us were nearly washed into the sea by the waves as they broke over the deck. Many times we were between two walls of water about six feet high on each side. We felt like the children of Israel must have felt when they crossed the Red Sea, only we had several hundred feet of water under our boat instead of dry land. The ocean in that area was over three thousand feet deep.

"We were drenched from head to foot. We had no dry clothes with us, since we had planned to return in the evening to Cebu Island, where we had left our car.

"Throughout the trip, however, we were not too fearful, for we believed that God wanted those New Testaments in the hands of the students on Bantayan Island.

"After more than two-and-a-half hours we approached the pier at Santa Fe on the western tip of the island only to find the waves were so high that they were breaking clear over the pier, making it impossible to land without wrecking the boat and probably losing our cargo.

"We decided to throw out the anchor over the stern and slow up the boat to land as near the beach as possible, keeping the boat headed into the wind. The only problem was that because of the high winds and the heavy surf the anchor would not hold, and about thirty feet from the shore we ran aground.

"With some help from men on shore we carried the boxes of New Testaments on our heads through the surf to the beach. Many times the men almost lost their footing in the heavy surf, but the boxes were all unloaded safely, and although some of the boxes got wet, the Scriptures were all kept dry. We were thankful for the way they had been packed with double corrugated board.

"We loaded the New Testaments in a jeepney and drove to the first high school, already far behind schedule. We were soaking wet, dirty, and hungry.

"We visited all the high schools in the three towns on Bantayan Island during the rest of the day and placed 2,400 Scriptures in the hands of teachers and students. We were told that this was the largest amount of Scriptures they had ever had on the island.

"The storm lasted all day and on through the night. The next day we took the launch back to the mainland on Cebu Island. We arrived back at port safely with mission accomplished!"

But schools and universities were not the only places that felt the impact of Charlie's faithful witness. Frequently he was called upon to lecture regarding the agriculture problems and possibilities of the country. He would say, "As we sit here, it is difficult to realize that today ten thousand children in this world will die from malnutrition. Tomorrow ten thousand more will die, and so on for each day of the remainder of this year. One million babies will be born that have to be fed and clothed.

"Food production is the responsibility of those who are engaged in agriculture; yet we cannot keep pace with a population in the world of nearly 3½ billion people, and this will increase by 1980 to over 5 billion people.

"Each year the world is falling behind in food production.

"Of all the countries in the Orient, the Philippines has the greatest future in agriculture. We have problems, but we have the land, the water, and the people to enable us to produce large enough amounts of food to serve our needs and also to share with others. To increase our production is our responsibility under God.

"Agriculture is the oldest vocation known to man. We read in the Bible that God himself planted the first garden eastward in Eden. We read also that God liked to walk in the garden in the cool of the evening.

"Agriculture is directly related to definite laws that God established when this world was created. Without these laws, we could not exist. God has promised seed time and harvest, and we are told that a seed to reproduce must be planted in the ground and die, if a new crop is to be born.

"When God planted the first garden he created a man to care for it. He put the plants and animals in families. In hybridizing, we must follow those family lines.

"Irrigation plays a very important part in agriculture. We must learn to conserve the water that God gives us so abundantly." Then Charlie would tell his listeners about the living water, Christ, provided by God for their thirsty souls.

Mayors of cities asked Charlie to speak at their Rotary Club luncheons and elsewhere. "One mayor said to me, 'What is wrong with Cortobato City? We have a murder about every week.'

"At first I was puzzled about this invitation to speak," Charlie says, "but then God gave me the answer. When I got up to speak to those men I said to them, 'The trouble with your city is sin, and the answer is Christ.'

"I was asked, after that, to bring the same message to many cities."

But Harriet was busy, too. There were Bible classes for girls and a women's ministry; she also started a beauty shop. Often she accompanied Charlie on his long island treks. They had an unusual ministry and an open door to work among the Muslims and in prisons on the various islands.

"Harriet's ministry was very unusual," Charlie says. "The Good Shepherd Sisters wanted to start a home for wayward girls between the ages of ten and sixteen years. These were girls who had been picked up by the police in Cebu City. The Sisters wanted to give these girls an opportunity to straighten out their lives and to be useful to society.

"The Sisters started this home for girls in a rented house. Because Harriet was a mother and understood girls, they asked her to teach the girls Bible and etiquette. The girls were in the home under police sentence for two years. In the meantime the city allotted some property for a permanent home. I was able to help design the home, which was then built to take care of thirty-five girls. We soon realized that we needed to do more than give them textbook knowledge, and therefore we built a modern poultry operation where they could learn poultry raising and marketing.

"Then Harriet started classes in sewing and cooking, which helped to train the girls. Our next project was gardening. This worked out well, because the girls liked to raise vegetables.

"Still we felt that they needed a project where they could learn a trade. In talking it over with the Sisters, we thought that a modern beauty parlor would be worthwhile. We have friends in Los Angeles, Mr. and Mrs. Carl Olson, who had a wholesale beauty supply business. We wrote them and they agreed to make a gift to the Cebu Girls' Center of a complete beauty shop with modern equipment."

Charlie would frequently apologize for his long letters. Page after page would be filled with a report of the busyness of their long days, the difficult traveling conditions, the new and varied experiences, the adjustments to food, climate and living conditions—but through it all one sensed the contagion of excitement and joy that was theirs. There were not enough hours in the day to do all the things they wanted to do. They couldn't get around fast enough; they needed more Bibles and Testaments. Charlie and Harriet were happy in the service of the King in their "Mission of Helps," as they came to call what they were doing.

After reading a five-page letter in single-spaced typing to the "dear ones at home," you can almost hear Charlie pausing just enough to catch his breath as he looks over what he's written, decides it is long enough, and then adds a postscript: "Please excuse mistakes. My typewriter doesn't spell so good!"

When it came time to leave he had visited almost every island in the Philippines, as well as the countries of Indonesia, South Vietnam, Cambodia, Taiwan, Thailand, and Korea. Wherever he went he was asked to hold agricultural seminars. The Gideons, in describing his work, said he wasn't horsing around with pleasantries but making every minute count for the Lord, which indeed he was.

And then it was time to come home. Charlie sat at his old typewriter and wrote a letter to His Excellency, Ferdinand E. Marcos, president of the Republic of the Philippines. The letter was dated February 29, 1972. "Five years ago Mrs. Barrows and I came to the Philippines at your invitation to serve as consultants in agriculture. During this time I have had the privilege of working with many of your leaders in agriculture and have learned to love your country and your people. . . .

"The time has come when we feel that we should go home to visit our family and to celebrate our fiftieth wedding anniversary.

"Our prayers will continue to be that as the president of this republic, God will give you wisdom, understanding, and purpose."

What Charlie left unsaid could be read between the lines. Both he and Harriet had left a part of their hearts on the islands.

Once back in the States the Barrows moved into a home in Turlock, California. Harriet unpacked the shells she had been accumulating in their travels—each shell brought back a memory.

But Charlie was not content to sit in a rocking chair. Once again he plunged into Gideon work. He had been showing Worldwide Films all over the islands, and now he made himself available to do that in this country. Speaking engagements poured in from all over. One month his calendar was crowded with twenty meetings. He made frequent trips to other parts of the Orient, attempting to get into Burma and other difficult places. His heart ached as he saw the devastation in Vietnam and witnessed the suffering of the people.

In January 1975 he wrote of his hopes to eventually get into China. "It is hard for me to sit still," his letter stated. "There is so much to do and, for me, too little time left to do my share. I am thankful for good health and for plenty of ambition even at the age of seventy-four. Harriet is well and very busy. She too has many irons in the fire."

In closing he said, "So goes the world for us, with much to be thankful for and much expectation as to what our Lord has planned for us next."

In the summer of 1976 he wrote me stating that once again he would be heading back to the Orient. "I suppose at my age I ought to have sense enough to stay home and take it easy, but Burma, Taiwan, and the Philippines still tug at my heart, and I feel I should go back and visit the brethren."

The first time I met Charlie and Harriet Barrows, Charlie related something to me that has explained to my satisfaction the motivating force in their lives. "Dr. Louis Talbot had a motto over his desk which read 'El Shaddi.'

"I said to him, 'What does that mean?'

" 'It's very simple,' Dr. Talbot answered, 'it means the God who is big enough.'

"I've taken that for my life motto. When someone says to me, 'Charlie, what do you think God can do in this situation?' I'll say, 'He can do anything. He's big enough!'

"There are no problems that God can't handle, young lady," Charlie said as he looked at me that day. "That made a strong impression on me early in life, and I've never forgotten it. And don't you forget it," he added as he stretched out his hands in an upward gesture, "El Shaddi—He's a God who is big enough!"

Pat and Shirley Boone and their daughters

2
The Carpenter's Helper

ENTERTAINER
PAT BOONE

"Pat Boone and his wife are on location in one of the lettuce fields. I'll be seeing them to gather information for a chapter in a book I'm doing."

I was telling this to some co-workers. Salinas, California is known as the salad bowl of the world, and we were living there at the time the Boones were filming television commercials. The reply from one of the men in the office brought howls of laughter: "He'll get his white shoes dirty."

The laughter was suggestive of ridicule. The undertones of both the statement and the laughter did not escape me. Later, as I left the television studio, one of the fellows called after me, "Don't step on his white bucks!"

The "Mr. Clean" image that Pat Boone conveys is well known. I asked Pat's secretary, Janet Fix, how Pat and Shirley reacted to such comments.

"The white bucks have been with Pat for so long, that he takes it all in stride, as does Shirley. He has always been known for his strong religious beliefs and has had the Mr. Clean image. Somehow, the white bucks have come to symbolize this clean image, and, probably because both Pat and

Shirley know that the world just doesn't understand, they don't let it bother them. I guess because they have such a confident attitude toward themselves now, and their standing with the Lord, this kind of ridicule runs off quite quickly."

Of the epithets thrown at him through the years, all bearing an astonishingly familiar ring, Pat himself says, "I laugh now, but there was a time when I was cringing. Although they're really compliments, they cast me in the role of a square, a guy just a little bit out of the mainstream of life."

When did Pat Boone stop cringing? "The day I discovered something more important to me than my public image, or anything else—my relationship with the most significant person in all history, Jesus."

For as long as he can remember, Pat was aware of God. "My first recollections of the religious side are of church in Donelson, Tennessee, which I attended weekly with my parents and my brother, Nick, and sisters, Margie and Judy.

"As a family we prayed at the table and had devotionals. As a boy alone in the woods or riding on my bike, I thought about God, and I talked to him and came to him with specific requests. The Bible's precepts were the way of life for us as a family—God expected us to love each other, to tell the truth, and not to cheat or steal. Right was right, and wrong was wrong. I was taught that the Bible could provide answers to all of the problems I would face in life.

"Jesus Christ was also very real to me in those years. What Jesus did and said not only solved the problems of the people of his day but also made sense to me in mine. It was shortly before my thirteenth birthday that I decided to commit my life to Christ."

Between that time and the present, Pat Boone rose from singing for milkshakes at the Belle Meade Theater to becoming one of the country's all-time top stars. But in his thirty-fourth year, after wearing the Mr. Clean label and bearing the brunt of jokes about it from such entertainer friends as Dean Martin, Phil Harris, Andy Williams, Frank Sinatra,

Entertainer Pat Boone

the Laugh-In gang, and others and inwardly cringing while outwardly laughing, Pat was able to feel all right about it. He explains: "Up to that time I had been just a churchman paying, as it were, my dues. I wasn't claiming the promises that Jesus makes in the Bible to those who really believe in him and commit their all to him. I knew a lot about Christ—when I finally met him, however, Jesus became as alive to me as he was two thousand years ago when he walked the dusty roads of Galilee. And when you experience his living presence—not just intellectually but in your very spirit—you know it. And so my life changed."

The change came about as a result of an "excruciating, soul-searching, God-seeking effort" he admits. "Every crevice of my life has felt the great joy and the overcoming power that the living Jesus brings," he says with that well-known radiant smile. As he speaks, you sense the faith, the hope, and the confidence that are hallmarks of this man's character.

My first encounter with Pat Boone was at a luncheon in the penthouse offices of Edward Johnson in 1973. (Mr. Johnson's story appears elsewhere in this book.) Pat's presence caused quite a stir. But Pat, I have since come to realize, does not intentionally come on the scene with the idea of creating a stir. He is as down to earth and as unaffected by stardom and fame as anyone can possibly be.

My second meeting with Pat was in his Beverly Hills office—an executive suite that is attractive and well appointed but certainly not overdone. I was again impressed with his naturalness, his casual mannerisms, his way of putting you at ease. He has often been described as having a boyish charm and as being an influential big-brother figure. Those are not inaccurate descriptions. Like a biblical predecessor of whom Jesus said, "He is without guile," I saw Nathaniel-like qualities in Pat Boone.

I questioned his secretary about these character traits, which I had observed with such consistency each time we

25

met. It also came through in his correspondence. "Doesn't he have any glaring faults?"

Janet, who knows Pat and Shirley as well as anyone, wrote back: "Both Pat and Shirley have great humility, though they are very aware of who they are, of their importance and position. There are some areas where I suppose one could find fault, but their assets far outweigh their liabilities. Pat's quiet, humble attitude comes quite naturally and honestly because of his upbringing. His parents are beautiful people. They are soft-spoken, gentle, and very loving. They were strict disciplinarians.

"I really believe that Pat is one of the most consistent Christians I know. He is always manifesting the fruit of the Spirit in his life.

"I've often said that Pat's greatest vice is also his greatest virtue. That is, he's too nice. Consequently, some of us often have to get him out of situations."

But Pat would be the first to admit that at one time he was one of the world's biggest hypocrites. "I was trying to live in two worlds, but the more I tried, the more I found myself pulled apart. It's downright painful to have to admit this, and I'd much rather leave unsaid and untold the failures and flaws that I kept hidden for so many years, but I must confess to great failure and inadequacy at a period of time in my life because I want to recount God's love and faithfulness. Thank God, when I finally admitted these things to him, he restored me into fellowship with him. And when I gave him back a life and a career that I had thoroughly messed up, he drew me into a greater and more wonderful relationship to him than I have ever dreamed possible."

Pat Boone calls the transformation in his life "an incredible, priceless swap. The most preposterously unequal trade in creation . . ."

But Pat almost missed out on the transaction when he was bartering an eternity in heaven with the God of all creation for fleeting fame and fun here on this planet earth.

The Boones were high school sweethearts at David Lipscomb High School in Nashville, Tennessee. Marriage came during Pat's initial year at David Lipscomb College, where the beautiful daughter of the all-time-great country-and-western singer, Red Foley, became his wife.

A year later they moved to Denton, Texas, where Pat enrolled in North Texas State Teachers College. Of those days he says, "The events that followed during our time in Texas were great experiences on which to draw in later years. I've often wondered, if God had not been so real to us then would we ever have been able to weather the tumultuous years that followed in Hollywood, when our faith almost disappeared? We were young and headstrong, but God gave us some exhilarating, faith-building experiences."

Can readers picture the Pat Boone of today working at Fort Worth's WBAP-TV as a singer and bringing home a $44.50 weekly paycheck?

While in Texas the first of Pat and Shirley's four daughters was born. It was at this time that Pat made his initial recording debut with "Two Hearts," a single, which was an immediate success. This was followed by his first million seller, "Ain't That a Shame."

The Boones took this life of faith up to New York City in 1954. Subsequent to this Pat won honors on the "Ted Mack Amateur Hour" and the "Arthur Godfrey Talent Scout Show." The invitation came from Godfrey for Pat to appear on his show as a regular while Pat was also attending Columbia University in New York.

Success was meteoric. "The pace of our lives quickened. I was going to Columbia full time, and three more daughters had been born into our family. Although we did have the normal tensions, pressures, and problems that come from a busy schedule, somehow the excitement of recording sessions, the Godfrey Show, television specials, and new babies kept us close together."

In 1956, 20th Century-Fox signed Pat to a million dollar

contract, and in succeeding years he starred in fifteen motion pictures, including such box-office hits as *Bernardine, April Love, All Hands on Deck, Mardi Gras,* and *Yellow Canary.* That same year the American Broadcasting Company signed him to his first television series, "The Pat Boone Chevy Showroom." At that time he had the distinction of being the youngest performer on television with his own network show. There were other television shows and appearances, all of which were adding up to make Pat Boone one of the country's most popular up-and-coming personalities.

"Things happened breathtakingly fast," he says. "During this period Shirley trusted me to come up with right answers, and together we looked to God for them. Sometimes we'd find them in the Bible; other times they came in answer to prayer. As a result of all that was happening, Shirley had me on a pedestal. We were involved in church but, despite this happy influence, in the late 1950s I was more and more taken up with my career. Its involvements were new and different. The new friends I made also were different; their objectives in life were certainly not the same as mine."

In 1958 Pat's desire for learning was fulfilled when he graduated magna cum laude from Columbia University. Pat credits Shirley for encouraging him to reach this educational milestone.

Thus began a new era in Pat Boone's life—a time of living a dual kind of existence. "I became one sort of person to the people who were becoming increasingly important to the success of my career, while I tried to remain the old Pat Boone to my wife Shirley."

This was when the Pat Boone image of the nice clean all-American boy-next-door began to develop. "As the opportunity to do motion pictures came along, this was the image I portrayed in films," he says.

Before leaving New York in 1960 to move to California, ten more gold records with over a million sales each were recorded. The reader may remember "Anastasia," "Love Letters In the Sand," "Friendly Persuasion," "April Love," and "Wonderful Time Up There."

Of this epic time in his career, Pat says, "Had I known then what the future would hold in the next five years, I might have melted down the gold records and quit while I was ahead."

The move to the West Coast was prompted by his decision to concentrate on movies and quit the grind of weekly television performances. At this time the film *Journey to the Center of the Earth* was made.

There was a gradual shift in standards. "Shirley saw that I moved with equal ease from a Hollywood cocktail party to a church pulpit. I switched from one to the other, laying down one set of standards and picking up another as the occasion demanded."

When Shirley confronted Pat with these things, comparing the new Pat Boone with the Pat and the family life they used to have, Pat was evasive and compromising. "Look," he told her, "we all change. We've got to change. We can't always be naïve children."

But, though he wouldn't admit it, Pat's biggest problem at that time was himself. Whereas before there had been a beautiful togetherness in their relationship and the things they enjoyed doing, now Pat went his separate way. Shirley doubted his dedication and leadership even while Pat insisted on the family dutifully attending church. "I became used to some people thinking I was hypocritical; inwardly, of course, I knew I *was* hypocritical, and that I was not so committed to the Lord as I ought to be. I had gotten to the point where I was trying to balance the life of an entertainer with that of a Christian. I felt like I was neither fish nor fowl and I was miserable. . . . I knew I was a compromiser."

By 1960 Pat Boone was one of the top ten names in show business. He had thirteen gold records, seven gold albums, five major motion pictures, his own television show, and he was a millionaire. A miserable millionaire.

"The debilitating thing about compromises, of course, is that one leads to another," Pat cautions.

Communication between the Boones became increasingly difficult. The marriage became shaky. Rumors of dissension started flying in Hollywood. Shirley was labeled a spoilsport.

Upon the urging of "friends" and in a last-ditch effort to save their marriage, Shirley now joined the hard-partying beautiful people of Beverly Hills and Hollywood. But it was a false gaiety. The new swinging image that Shirley Boone tried to project left her sick physically and emotionally as she vainly tried to rationalize her way through the maze.

"It was a twisting, bumpy, downhill road," Pat says, "as we faced the spiritual crisis of our lives."

"Honey," Shirley announced one day, "I'm not going to nag you anymore," and with that statement she surrendered her convictions for a time. "I only want to remind you that you're taking five other souls with you wherever you go." In reflection, Pat says today, "It had an almost theatrical ring . . . but Shirl's statement came like a solar plexus blow."

On top of everything else, not unexpectedly—oftentimes a loving Father-God has to send us sprawling before we will look up—Pat's career was traveling a rocky road. "My marriage, my career, my children—please, God—why, God?" Pat was once again calling out. "I was at the bottom," he says, "with nowhere to look but up."

It was at that point that Clint Davidson walked into the Boones' lives. "He was a giant influence on me. His quiet, radiant confidence in God prepared me for the revelation that was to change the whole direction of my life." The end result was that a stirring in Pat's mind and heart began to take place.

Pat was now calling out to God, but in a new conversational way. On one occasion he found tears rolling down his cheeks as he refocused his thoughts on the recognition that

God was able to do things that ability, intellect, and experience cannot do. There was an indefinable longing to experience something of the miraculous in his life as the biblical people had, as Clint Davidson and his wife had.

About this time Pat became interested in Dave Wilkerson's book *The Cross and the Switchblade* and the book's movie possibilities. Then businessman George Otis crossed his path. Unflinchingly Otis pointed out that it would be very difficult for Pat to play the part of Wilkerson until he came to know the Holy Spirit in the same way the author of the book knew him.

Wilkerson's prayers had been answered in specific and supernatural ways. Pat's antenna went up. Hadn't Wilkerson consistently risked his life in the ghettos of New York on the proposition that God performs miracles today? His story, as told in the book, was crammed with answered prayer, changed lives, and healings.

Davidson, Wilkerson, Otis were each tremendously successful, each speaking of a relationship with Christ that supercharged their lives.

Otis gave Pat a box of stereotape cartridges on which the New Testament in modern language was recorded. Driving to and from his home, Pat found himself flipping on a Bible tape. "Whenever I listened, a sort of peace drifted into the car, despite crowded traffic. My Ferrari became a virtual sanctuary."

But with Shirley Boone it was now a different story. Home was no longer a sanctuary. The ragged nerve-endings of her private agony finally drove her to her knees, sobbing, confessing to God that her love for her husband was slipping from her. A grayness was settling in. She started reading books on spiritual themes; she took a greater interest in church activities and spent more time with Christian people. The bleakness of her spirit sent her searching. Because we have a prayer-hearing and a prayer-answering God, he responded to Shirley's pleas. One evening her longing was climaxed at a church service where she heard a message on total commitment to Jesus Christ. In desperation, when the invitation came she struggled to her feet and felt an irresistible desire to kneel. For the first time in many months, Shirley Boone discovered that God was as near as her own heartbeat. In the months that followed, the relationship deepened as she searched the Scriptures for a better understanding of God, his Son, and the work of the Holy Spirit.

As Shirley read the Bible she began to see that the Holy Spirit was as personal as God and Jesus Christ. She came to learn that when you know the Holy Spirit, he gives you a love for people that you can't understand or explain. Romans 5:5 became alive for her "because the love of God has been poured out within our hearts through the Holy Spirit who was given to us."

An awareness of the Holy Spirit as being the third person of the Godhead was invading both Pat and Shirley's lives. Now she was hungrily reading the Bible, devouring it and, what's more, understanding it.

"What we both wanted now was more of a sense of direction, more faith. Both of us were groping and searching. I knew that Paul had said in Romans 10:17 that 'faith comes by hearing the Word of God.' We were doing that literally. An expectancy was growing. Was it hope?"

A merciful God took the Boone's hope and turned it into faith. Later, Pat was to read in the book of Hebrews these words: "Now faith is the assurance of things hoped for, the conviction of things not seen" (Heb. 11:1) and recognize that this is what God had done for them.

It was while Pat was away on some appearances, on a summer day in 1968, that Shirley, with the help of two friends, Merlyn Lund and George Otis, began a search in the Bible to seek out the teachings regarding the person of the Holy Spirit. Later, after these friends left, alone in her bedroom, Shirley opened her heart to God in an earnest desire to praise him, and heard herself speaking with a freedom of expression she'd never thought humanly possible. "I was overcome by the sense of the presence of the Lord," she explains, "and the amazing thing that happened to me was that I felt myself immersed in love."

The afterglow of peace and well-being that followed was indescribable. "The change in Shirley was immediate," Pat says.

The enemy of our souls does not leave us alone when God is doing something in our lives. Shirley was to feel the cunning of Satan and his power to deceive. Both Pat and Shirley needed confirmation that this beautiful language was truly a gift of God's Spirit. God gave them this assurance in a miraculous way. One night as Shirley was drifting into sleep, Pat overheard her whispering. He listened closely, intrigued, transfixed. "My wife was praising the Lord in Latin. I knew she had never had a day of Latin, but I had studied it for four years. Yet she now was saying very distinctly, 'Ava Deum! Ava Deum!' or 'Praise God' in a language she'd never learned. The Holy Spirit gave Shirley a phrase that he knew I could interpret for our mutual faith and edification."

There was another gift from God. "He returned in rich abundance the lost love that Shirley had for me. I also felt a greater love for Shirley than I had for many months. From that moment until now, love that was dying has continually blossomed into an even richer and more beautiful relationship. The tender Spirit of the living Lord has given increasing dimensions to our love for each other, for our children, and for every other child of God. Now we began to understand what Paul was saying when he spoke of the 'fruit of the Spirit' (Gal. 5:20).

"This new capacity for love, as well as the other 'fruit of the Spirit' in our daily lives, proves to us even more than the prayer language that Jesus' own Spirit is truly dwelling in us."

Seeing his wife transformed from a frustrated and confused woman into a beautiful Christian personality radiating peace and joy, devotion to Christ, love for him and their daughters, a passion for the Bible, and a deep concern for others' problems was a profoundly moving experience for Pat Boone. "Her 'newness of life' was the greatest testimony of all. And there were others we were meeting, usually in Bible studies and in prayer groups. I could see that these people had been with Jesus, and feel in them the power and joy that was real. I wanted this."

Along about this time, total financial disaster threatened the Boone household. In an interview on June 1, 1973, *Forbes* magazine quoted him as saying, "I have the reverse Midas touch. Everything I touch turns to zilch" (p. 66). With the Oakland Oaks (one of his investments) and a string of other interests exploding in his face, Pat Boone found himself at the lowest emotional ebb in his life.

It was in January of 1969, after seeking the help of topflight lawyers and financial experts, that Pat came to the conclusion that although the financial people could offer advice and suggestions, "only God was going to solve the problem. And I knew I couldn't expect him to solve this problem unless I belonged totally to him." Thus with all the barriers down, totally yielded, and before the open Bible, as he came to the account of Peter responding to Jesus and walking on the water (Matt. 14), Pat Boone knew that he, too, like Peter, had to go to Jesus.

"O Father, this is it—I give up. I yield my life to you. Please take it, Lord, and make it whatever you want to. Forgive me of every sin, wash me clean; and Jesus, oh, precious Jesus, be my Baptizer." Even as Pat prayed he sensed the Lord's presence in a tender way and he began to sing a beautiful melody with strange Hebraic words. "How can you describe such a thing?" he asks. "It was an uplifting, inspiring, joyful experience. I had a deep sense of knowing that I was singing a new song to God."

In the days that followed, Pat and Shirley witnessed an amazing demonstration of God's answers to their prayers as

God confirmed his reality to their daughters in completely individualized ways suited to the temperament and needs of the girls. "Our family life took on an enormously exciting dimension," he relates.

The need to maintain his career and provide for his family was still there, but now Pat was remembering Jesus' promises. "Thank the Lord, I know I'm not at the mercy of anybody or anything. I'm on the winning team! My responsibility is to read the Word of God, find out what it says, and then by faith, believe and act upon what he promised."

This Pat did. His confidence in the Holy Spirit's guiding presence grew. As he sought God's forgiveness for getting himself into his financial predicament, he also asked for future guidance. The miraculous did not occur overnight, but as Pat and his believing, praying friends and family thanked God for deliverance, Pat was able to say, "The bank is in the hands of God. He will provide." And God did. "It was a fantastic answer to prayer," Pat says. "There is no other explanation."

Since these events, magazines have been quick to pick up on what has happened to Pat and his family. Many of the articles have not been complimentary. As his secretary sees it, to nonbelievers, Pat is unbelievable. "People think that no one can be that good, that nice, that religious, except as a gimmick."

But the Boones' faith is real. Both Pat and Shirley know that darkness cannot comprehend light, and they understand and accept the chiding from scoffers and disbelievers.

It was after a tour of Japan in 1971, which had included all the Boone family, that it was decided that a professional union of the Boones could be extremely successful. That year the Boones recorded their first family album. Since then there have been a number of others. In addition, the family has performed in the concert circuit around the world. Pat says, "We call this entertainment with a plus. Over the last several years, I've been trying to find ways to gracefully blend contemporary music with the Gospel message. It's not always easy, but I think the goal is more than worth stretching for." The popularity of Pat and his family shows that the effort has been appreciated and well worthwhile.

Success in the entertainment industry has been aptly described as a very elusive commodity. It is also said that the key to success in show business is not so much reaching stardom but maintaining it. This Pat Boone has done.

It is estimated that he has sold well over fifty million records since the beginning of his recording career. He has recorded approximately sixty albums and three hundred singles.

No other Christian family, it is believed, has appeared on national television as often as Pat and Shirley and their daughters, Cherry, Lindy, Debby, and Laury. In 1975 the two oldest Boone girls were married. Pat's secretary, Janet, says: "They have maintained their standards for dating and authority throughout the girls' engagements. Frankly, some of us who know them well thought they were overly strict in enforcing rules they established years ago, but they have been consistent and the girls have respected them for it and obeyed. Lindy appeared on Phil Donahue's show opposite Christy Hefner (daughter of Hugh Hefner of *Playboy* magazine). They had a discussion about premarital sex. Lindy did exceptionally well and upheld biblical standards with great authority and sincerity. So you can see, the parents' teaching has sunk in." *Christian Life* magazine (April 1976) carried a very informative exclusive interview with Pat, in which he discusses how he raised his girls. Pat and Shirley have maintained discipline—a loving authority—over the girls, and Pat says, "It has made a tremendous difference in our family life and in the girls' feeling of well-being and security."

Of the Boone family life, Janet says: "The family has always been exceptionally close, sharing a lot of togetherness. When all the girls were in school, they always had breakfast together, with Bible reading, hymn singing, and prayers before they left the house. The older they got and the more varied the schedules, the more difficult it became to gather in the morning—but always, some time during the day, they have a family worship.

"Again, when the girls were younger and I was living with them, when 9:00 P.M. came around (the bedtime for the youngest) it was time for everyone to gather in the master bedroom for prayers. And it wasn't just prayers—often there was a real sense of worship, praise, and ministry to one another.

"Pat and Shirley have been very careful to be home for special occasions—for the girls' school functions, and for birthdays. I've known Pat to turn down fairly important engagements so he could be home to see one of the girls perform in a school play or to be there for a birthday or graduation. It's a very close family, and the girls tell their parents everything. Cherry has been known to say that she considers her parents her best friends."

When I asked Pat how such a busy man as he managed to maintain a devotional life, he replied by stating that he begins the day in prayer, "sometimes before I even get out of bed. As soon as I become conscious and awake I often begin to just talk to the Lord to thank him for the new day and my health and the things that come to my mind first. After I get up and have some Bible reading and devotional with whichever of the girls are up and Shirley, some of us will take a brisk walk and talk to the Lord and praise him as we go."

How does he handle his time and the demands made upon him? "I'm not a good one to ask for hints on wise use of time, because I keep cramming more things into a day than I can possibly get done. They overlap and I'm often late. But I do know that the days when I really ask the Lord's guidance on the use of my time and spend more time with him in the

Word and in prayer, those days go more smoothly and I can look back on a much better day. It is easy to let our days get cluttered and chaotic."

What are some of the things Pat Boone wrestles with personally? "I guess one of the major things I wrestle with, and most of us do, is how to hear the voice of the Lord, and to know what his will is, particularly when it comes to dividing my time between professional things—singing, television, records—and more direct ministry opportunities."

"I feel that every Christian is meant to be salt, that is, to get in and flavor and change and preserve the areas that he's directly involved in. In my case, that's entertainment and the use of media—communication. Of course, I have ample opportunity to do that, and I've brought my own family into the picture.

"Many Christians write saying I should get out of what they consider secular entertainment and get into direct ministry or evangelism. We have been led to see that ministry and evangelism should be part of whatever one does, whether it's selling insurance or keeping house or pumping gas, not just filling a pulpit or conducting crusades. I especially lean on Paul's admonition in I Corinthians 7 that 'a man should remain in the vocation in which he's called.' In other words, 'Bloom where you are planted.' I really believe that the Lord wants dedicated, Spirit-filled Christians in every walk of life, on every level of responsibility, and claiming those areas where he works and lives as Kingdom territory. So that's what I'm trying to do as a singer, entertainer, and author.

"More and more I see that if I will just keep myself submitted to him in tune with his will for me personally, in devotion and submission and in learning his Word, that he will use the opportunity I have as a person and as an entertainer, in ways I could never foresee.

"Allow God to help you 'grow up' in the faith. Ask him to

show you how to minister to others, how to understand his Word, how to cultivate and practice the other gifts, how to praise and serve him better and better. I believe God wants us to walk a day at a time and a step at a time without seeing his overall plan. What a life! What a Savior! What a victorious destiny we can all have! And it's already begun because we're in Jesus, and he is in us!"

Leighton and Jean Ford

3
A Man with a Burden

EVANGELIST
LEIGHTON FORD

January, 1949; Chatham, Ontario, Canada. The date and place are etched into his mind. He remembers looking over the auditorium and silently thanking the Lord for the full house. In spite of the cold and the snow falling steadily, people came to hear the young evangelist from the States. Seventeen-year-old Leighton Ford had worked hard to help put together this youth rally and his expectations were high. Surely this was the night when hearts would be touched and people's lives changed as they moved in response to the Holy Spirit speaking through the young evangelist Billy Graham. As he listened and watched, he recalled how his own heart had been deeply stirred at a Youth for Christ Rally where Billy Graham had been the speaker. That had been his first introduction to the youthful evangelist, and he recognized that here was a man destined to be mightily used by the Lord.

But now the meeting was over. The altar call had been given and Leighton stood numb in disbelief. Where were all the people? "Hardly anybody came forward to accept Christ," he relates as he recalls the meeting. "I was terribly disappointed and stood there silently weeping over the slim response to the invitation. All of a sudden I felt strong but gentle arms around my shoulders. It was Billy. 'Leighton,' he said to me, 'God has given you a burden. And God always blesses the man with a burden.' "

The then-unknown Billy Graham comforted the younger man with his presence and his words. A bond was formed in that moment, a bond born out of mutual love for Christ and compassion for the world's lost, a bond that was to increase through the years and become even more special and meaningful in the marvelous outworking of God's perfect plan for each of their lives.

As evangelist Dr. Leighton Ford sat in his Charlotte, North Carolina, home sharing these memories, at his side was a trim little blond who bears a striking resemblance to Dr. Billy Graham. Leighton's wife, Jean, could not conceal her great respect and love for the man with whom she has shared her life since their first meeting in 1951.

"I was planning to go to the University of Toronto," Leighton explained, "but Billy told me about Wheaton College, which he had attended, and encouraged me to think about that, and so I did. I learned more about it, applied there, and Billy gave me a good recommendation, so I ended up there."

The petite blond who presides over the lovely Ford home is, of course, the youngest sister of Billy Graham. "Billy told me all about this fellow he met in Canada," Jeanie said with a twinkle in her big blue eyes. It would appear that big brother Billy was watching out for his little sister.

The meeting between the two was actually deliberately planned, and Leighton admitted to helping plot the occasion. "I'm blessed to be able to admit it now," he laughingly related, "but a close friend of mine was dating Jeanie and he said to me, 'This is the girl you ought to meet, Leighton,' so we set up a double date to go to a hockey game in Chicago. John dated Jeanie, and I dated another girl. But the motive behind the whole thing was so I could meet Jeanie."

"Shortly after that he asked me out on a date, and that turned out to be a disaster," Jean added.

Leighton picked up the story. "We were going to a concert and, because I showed up thirty minutes late, we weren't able to sit together."

"So when he asked for another date I was really surprised and I thought, 'Well, the first time was such a disaster, I'll go with him one more time so we can get to know each other on a little different level.'

"And on that second date we just fell desperately in love, both of us. We were coming back from a meeting in Chicago, and we stopped at a restaurant. He got me an orange drink, and just as he was handing it to me I looked at him, and he looked at me, and that was the way we fell in love."

"Exactly right," Leighton interrupted, "our eyes just sort of met and click, that was it."

The lovelight in their eyes for each other has never dimmed.

For the rest of the Wheaton school year Leighton and Jeanie were an inseparable couple. Leighton's reserved Canadian mannerisms were in contrast to the sparkling little southerner, but they soon discovered the many ways in which they complemented each other, and their love grew.

During his Wheaton years, Leighton was very active in what they called The Christian Council, speaking on Gospel teams. "We fanned out all over the Midwest during the school year, speaking at youth rallies and at church services, and then, in the summer, we went across the country. I sang in a trio and preached.

During the summer of 1952, after graduation from Wheaton, he served as a film representative for Billy's first dramatic film production, *Mr. Texas.*

In the fall of 1952 Leighton enrolled at Columbia Seminary, while Jean continued her schooling at Wheaton. "It was the end of 1952, on New Year's Eve, when I came to Charlotte and proposed to Jeanie just before midnight. We were married in December 1953."

"Billy married us," Jean stated, "along with two other ministers, Grady Wilson and the pastor of our church in Charlotte. Billy probably hadn't married over two or three other couples before that time, and he made so many mistakes, but one of the main ones was that he said in the middle of the ceremony, 'Now that Leighton and Jean have exchanged wings,' and then he said, 'Oh, I mean rings,' and then my other brother, Melvin, just burst out laughing. And this was a big formal eight o'clock wedding in Charlotte, so you can imagine." The two of them shook their heads as they recalled the event.

I could not help but think, as the Fords related their delightful story, that there is joy in knowing and serving Jesus. The psalmist phrased it rightly: "For the Lord God is a sun and shield: the Lord will give grace and glory: no good thing will he withhold from them that walk uprightly" (Ps. 84:11). Leighton and Jean's lives have been characterized by unswerving devotion to Christ and world evangelization in obedience to Jesus' great commission.

Where did this sense of urgency to reach out to a lost and dying world and share Jesus Christ come from? What influences were brought to bear on their lives that helped to shape their early decisions, which became their life commitment?

In both of their lives the influence of their mothers shows up very strongly. "My parents were both Anglicans," Leighton explained, "but my mother was the devout Christian in our family. My father was a nominal churchgoer until later in life when he came to know the Lord through the impact of my own ministry on his life.

"I was an only child—an adopted child. This has always made spiritual adoption very meaningful to me, because I remember how my mother told me when I was about twelve that I was adopted. But she told it in such a way that I felt this was a very special thing—they didn't have to have me, they chose me—and so the idea as taught in the Bible that we can be God's adopted children, that we are special to him, is very significant, understandably, to me.

"My father was a jeweler and mother worked with him. My earliest recollections are of the two of them working in this little store in Chatham, Ontario, Canada. I was raised as a small-city boy, which makes Jeanie's background and mine very different. My mother, I felt, was overly protective of me and we did not have relatives or friends we were close to, so I lived a fairly isolated life in terms of friends and family. As I got older, however, I made friends on my own in school.

"I was a good student and worked hard at my schooling. I had some musical inclinations and speaking abilities, which I put to good use in college. I suppose the one word that would best describe me in my more youthful years would be 'studious.'

"My mother read biographies to me of great evangelists and missionaries and always stressed, 'Leighton, God needs other men like these.'

"She also had a prayer bench in the upstairs hall and she prayed there and would have me pray with her. Sometimes this was annoying to me. I was a fairly typical boy, I guess, and would have enjoyed playing hockey or football instead. But this did teach me something about prayer.

"The home that I came from was unhappy, however, in some ways. In other ways there was a great deal of love shown by my mother, and there was material security. But as my mother grew older she began to be very distorted in her thinking and finally became emotionally ill. She was paranoid and suffered from delusions of persecution. She and my father began to argue a great deal over the store, business, and money. I remember hearing them verbally insult each other in the middle of the night in those earlier years.

"When I was fourteen my mother was going through one of the periods of great fear in her life. But, strangely enough, it was at this time in my life that the real turning point came. Even though my parents were torn by marital strife, they took me to the Blue Water Conference not far from our home in southwestern Ontario.

"Two things happened to me there. I had accepted Christ as a small boy at the Canadian Keswick Conference in a children's meeting, but I took this for granted and really didn't fully comprehend what had happened to me. But at the Blue Water Conference I noticed that the young people whom I met had a sense of dedication to the Lord. They were radiant. The way they talked about Christ, the way they prayed, the songs they sang—all this made me want to have that kind of relationship.

"Dr. Oswald Smith was the speaker there that week. His messages about World Missions made a deep impression on me, particularly a message that he brought on the morning watch. He told about how he walked up and down and prayed out loud, having found that this helped him to overcome nervousness and wandering thoughts. I remember going out in the woods and taking my Bible along and reading the Psalms and turning them into prayers and just walking up and down, back and forth. In this way, I, too, began to learn the reality of fellowship with God in a new way.

"All of this made the Lord real in my life in a deeper way than ever before. It was a preparation for what lay ahead of me when I returned home. That fall my mother had to be sent to western Canada and I was a very lonely, discouraged, and concerned boy. I was left much to myself. That fall in my hometown I began working with a series of youth rallies known as the Canadian Youth Fellowship. Evon Hedley was the field director, and he entrusted me with the responsibility of being president of this group. We had monthly youth rallies aimed at communicating the Gospel to the high school students in our county in Canada. It was through this activity that I became vitally interested in evangelism and first met Billy and heard him speak. I had felt before that time that God was calling me, but it was through a combination of these experiences that my life was really turned around."

And what of Jean's childhood and young girlhood days?

"I would imagine that almost everyone knows of the Graham family background by now," she laughingly commented. The worldwide fame of big brother Billy Frank, as Jean and other members of the family still call him, has thrust the Graham family into the media.

"My father was a dairy farmer who was up at 2:30 every morning to milk the cows. As both of my brothers, Melvin and Billy, got to the age where they could help, they did. Mother kept books for my father's dairy. We were a very close family. Running the dairy was demanding work, and my parents and brothers put in long hours.

"Faithfulness in church attendance was a must in our family, and we had family devotions in the den every evening. We were raised on Bible reading and memorization. Then everyone would get down on his knees and participate in family prayers. Those were certainly learning years in many, many ways."

The Grahams believed in stern discipline. "Mother never owned a book on child psychology, but she had the Bible. She believed in exercising the kind of discipline the Book of Proverbs speaks of."

This writer has spent time with Mrs. Graham in the lovely old family home in Charlotte. "My husband believed in those verses in Proverbs," Mrs. Graham stated. "Proverbs 29 verse 15 says, 'The rod and reproof give wisdom: but a child left to himself bringeth his mother to shame,' so my husband would use the belt when necessary and I had a hickory switch."

Mrs. Graham took God at his Word. Proverbs 22:6 told her: "Train up a child in the way he should go, And when he is old he will not depart from it." This she and her husband did, and they had the joy of seeing all four of their children walk in the way with the Lord.

"Leighton is as my very own son," she told me in August 1976. "He even resembles Billy Frank, you know." And indeed I had noticed that, as have others.

"Jeanie had bulbar polio when she was twelve," Mrs. Graham related, "and we came very close to losing her."

"It was quite an experience for a twelve-year-old to go through," Jean added.

"We were told she probably wouldn't live," Mother Graham said, "and the first forty-eight hours were the most critical."

"I remember it very vividly," Jeanie recalled. "I was quarantined and could not see anyone for three weeks. But I never will forget that at the end of three weeks Daddy walked into the hospital and gave the head nurse a ten-dollar bill, which back in 1944 was a lot of money, and then he picked me up and bodily carried me out, although I hadn't even been dismissed from the hospital.

"Daddy started me on an exercise program for the next several months that really helped me to recuperate. I have effects even now from polio, because it is still hard for me to swallow and, when I get very tired, it is hard for me to talk.

"I went to a country school system and later transferred to a city school and finally ended up at Wheaton."

"Jean was a tomboy," her mother revealed. "Her interests were playing baseball, football, basketball, milking cows, and hauling hay—doing all the things that a farm girl would do."

"You liked to go around with your daddy especially, didn't you?" Leighton Ford questioned his wife.

"Just loved to go with him. Every time I heard the back door slam and I knew daddy was going out to the field, that is exactly where I wanted to go. When I got to be about fourteen my folks told me that I was getting too old to act like a tomboy and that I couldn't go to the dairy any more. They limited me in the time I could spend in the fields, and that really upset and bothered me because that was exactly where I wanted to be. A part of that, however, I realize now, was just a complete devotion to my father. I wanted to be where he was."

Jean graduated from Wheaton College in 1953 with her major in Christian Education. "From there I worked with Billy and the team for about nine months, doing some of his office and secretarial work and traveling in three different crusades—Detroit, Michigan, Syracuse, New York, and Ashville, North Carolina."

Leighton had graduated from Wheaton in 1952, summa cum laude, scoring the highest in his major that anybody had achieved up until that time.

After a brief but beautiful Florida honeymoon, Leighton and Jean returned to Decatur, Georgia, where they lived for the next year and a half while Leighton completed his seminary work.

"The first evangelistic meetings I held were in the Annie Linlay Presbyterian Church in Anderson, South Carolina in 1953 while I was still in seminary," he reminisces. He also served as a summer student pastor at the Westminster Presbyterian Church in Springfield, Missouri, and traveled throughout the South preaching and holding evangelistic meetings on every opportunity that came his way.

Those were valuable learning experiences.

Graduation from Columbia came with Leighton graduating magna cum laude. In subsequent years he was to receive honorary doctorates from Houghton College and Gordon College. "He's had many honors bestowed on him," said Jean. And Leighton quickly added, "And I've had a lot of different failures too. I don't know where we'd start to tell about those.

"After seminary Billy invited Jeanie and me to come to Scotland where he had just held a crusade and to spend the summer preaching on the beaches and in churches, and there were other campaigns and evangelistic meetings. We did that during the summer of 1955.

"That fall Billy was going to hold a crusade in Toronto, Canada, which was my hometown. I asked if I could help with that, and he welcomed me. And now it's more than twenty years and Billy hasn't been able to get rid of me. Since that time I've been an associate Evangelist with the Billy Graham Team, and I am a vice-president of the Billy Graham Association.

"During the early years of my work with the association, I spent much time speaking at youth meetings and high school assemblies and did much personal counseling, speaking in factories, railway workshops in Toronto, and other places. These, too, were valuable learning experiences.

"Then I began holding crusades of my own and, with Billy's encouragement, developed a team of my own as part of the Billy Graham Association. Much of my ministry during the 1960s was going from coast to coast in the large cities of Canada, and in many of the smaller cities as well. The preaching overseas took me to Africa, Latin America, Europe, Australia and New Zealand. It was a joy to preach in every continent in the world to several million people. Along with that a media ministry developed. Many of our crusades have been televised.

"In the late 1960s (about 1969), Billy asked me to share the 'Hour of Decision' radio broadcast, and for the last several years we have alternated preaching every other week.

"Another area of ministry has come in the writing of a number of books and magazine articles."

One of the ministries that Leighton Ford has pioneered with God's blessing has been a daily one-minute inspirational feature that has appeared on as many as forty-five television stations across the country. How did it come about?

"A Christian newsman in Charlotte came to me one day and said, 'You know, when I'm through giving the news at night on TV it's usually so bad I want to say, 'Let's pray.' He went on to say that he couldn't do that, of course, but he added, 'You could, or Billy could.' So we developed the feature in which I gave a scriptural perspective on some personal or current event, some anniversary or holiday. This is shown in most places during local news program prime time. The idea is to show how the Word of God applies to every area of life, whether it's baseball or the bear market on Wall Street."

"Leighton has always been very studious," Jean said with obvious pride. "Intellectually he's got it," she grinned.

"Jeanie has more practical common sense than I'll ever have," he teased back at her. Now it was Leighton's turn to compliment his wife. "She's a people person—practical, outgoing, makes friends easily. She's totally unselfish and ever so thoughtful of others, more than anybody I've ever known. She's been the most wonderful wife to me. She has a balance of the independent and the dependent. I'm not sure how you can put those two together, but when I have to travel so much as an evangelist, she has had to keep things going at home and make decisions and be mother and daddy and keep the home going—which she really does not want to do on her own, but she is able to do it. She has been able to develop that, and yet at the same time when I come back she wants me to be the father and to take over.

"God has given my wife an excellent perceptive mind. Jeanie is interested in different things. She reads and knows what is going on in current events. She has the gift of teaching, and the gift of giving encouragement to people—she is a great encourager. She is also very honest with people. People know where they stand with my Jeanie without her being blunt and hurting them. She can see people's problems and help them face up to things, including myself, and without making you feel put down. This is a real gift of affirmation that God has given to her. She earns people's confidence.

"She teaches a Bible class of young mothers and wives in Charlotte, which has been a tremendous blessing. We complement each other to a great extent. She has her ministry too, and we share together often. If I am preparing a sermon or talk, Jeanie helps me. I'll sit down and go over it with her.

"I also do this, by the way, many times with our daughter Debbie, who is also now at Wheaton College. Deb has many of the same gifts that her mother has in terms of insight, intuition, and being a 'people' person.

"When I go over a talk with Jeanie, she will think of ways to make it very personal and give suggestions for practical application. At the same time, I'll go over Jeanie's teaching lessons or talks, and I'll help her organize it, think about how she can outline it, how to put the points logically in place. She and I share together very much in this way.

"In the home as well as the church, as husbands and wives we ought to help each other to develop our God-given gifts. We each have different gifts and we need to encourage each other.

"I enjoy helping Jeanie around the house. I don't think of this as being women's work. We just enjoy helping each other.

"We have tried to live our lives not in terms of roles but in terms of using the gifts that God has given to each one of us. I believe the husband ought to be the head of the home morally and spiritually and to take that responsibility, but we also ought to bring out each other's gifts.

"But our home—my relationship with Jeanie and our children—has been very, very important to me, because the home that I came from was very unhappy in some ways, as I have explained."

It was Jean's turn to elaborate on their relationship. "I'm sure you can tell from listening to us," she said happily, "that after more than twenty-three years of marriage we are still desperately in love. I wish I could be objective when I talk to you about my husband, and I will be as objective as possible, but I think after being in love with somebody for as long as I have been in love with Leighton, that it is going to be more subjective than objective.

"Leighton is a very unusual person because he does come from this background of being an only child with an overly protective mother who dominated him somewhat; and yet he comes into a marriage with me, into being a father of three children, as the most super father and husband that anybody could ever have.

"Leighton is intellectually oriented, much more so than I am. He learns probably more from books and reading than I do. I probably learn more from people than he does, and I think as we look at each other we do complement each other because his strengths are my weaknesses. Leighton's ability to communicate is a very unusual God-given ability—it doesn't matter if it's to a group of boys at a golf camp, or to a mass meeting, or to a civic club, or on television or radio—he communicates on so many different levels. He is interested in individuals whom God loves. No group is too small for him to speak to. He enjoys small group Bible studies, and he also enjoys preaching at the large crusade meetings.

"He is so good at helping me around the house when I need it. He hardly ever says no unless there is a real reason to say it. My husband is an extremely kind person toward me and the children—very compassionate and very understanding. He may get irritated, but he very seldom loses his temper. I can't remember ever seeing Leighton really angry to the point where he was not in control of a situation. I would have to say that little things irritate him more than big things.

"I remember when I first met Leighton that John Wesley White, who introduced us and who is now a member of the Billy Graham Team, told me, 'Jean, Leighton has a shell, but once you break through that shell I think you've got a friend for life.' And that is true—Leighton is a very loyal person. If somebody is down, my husband is always there to defend him. You will very, very seldom hear Leighton criticize anybody. My husband is a peacemaker in any crowd. I have learned so much from my husband. He always tries to see both sides of an issue, and he tries not to condemn. Regardless of a person's personality, Leighton will be kind and tolerant.

"I'm sure your readers will think that I believe my husband has no faults—but I'm sure he does. I think he tends to get impatient with people who perhaps have not done their homework for a particular situation. He himself prepares very carefully for everything he does, whether it is television, radio, preaching, large crowds, committee meetings, or whatever.

"My own life has been greatly enriched and helped because of my husband.

"A major turning point in my life came, however, while at Wheaton College when Dr. Harold Ockenga came and presented a series of lectures on the Holy Spirit. This really changed my way of thinking. Dr. Ockenga is a very intellectual person and these were academic lectures, yet for the first time I realized that the Holy Spirit was a real person and could make a difference in my life.

"There have been many spiritual ups and downs in my life. More often we, as Christians, are willing to talk about our ups. I have often been helped, however, by looking at what happened to Elijah on Mt. Carmel (I Kings 18 and 19). Elijah was certainly down in the dumps and he said, 'God let me die, I'm the only prophet left.' At that point an angel came to him and said, 'Arise and eat.' Later, after he went out in the strength of that, a still small voice told him, 'Look, there are seven thousand out there who have never bowed to Baal . . . I've got more work for you to do.'

"And I think there is a lesson in that for us. I know this has happened in my own life when I've really been physically exhausted. From that passage in I Kings, I see that God is saying, 'Get some rest, get some good food, get away if need be, take care of yourself a little bit more. There is more work to be done for me. I need you. I can use you.'

"So I thank God for the many opportunities he brings our way for sharing, and for me, as a woman, an outlet to serve him as well."

I asked Leighton what were some of the things he wrestled with personally. "I would say that I've had to wrestle with loneliness inasmuch as I travel so much. As I've indicated, my home life means so much to me because of my background, so traveling solo as I've had to do much of the time I've wrestled with discouragement as much as anything. But out of this, I've learned to take a look at my life and accept the gifts and opportunities that God has given to me.

"I think, too, that many of us when we get to the forties, go through a sort of middle-age crisis, so to speak. We begin to look at ourselves, our lives, our goals, and wonder what we have really accomplished. The enemy likes to get us to wondering about our effectiveness. I've never questioned the reality of the Gospel, but I have wondered about my own effectiveness as a communicator for the Lord. It was during one of those times, while in Tulsa, Oklahoma, just before I had to speak at the university, that the Lord gave me a verse that has helped to hold me steady. It was, 'Fear not, I am your shield, I am your exceeding great reward' (Gen. 15:1).

"The Lord said to me through that verse that results were not the important thing, nor whether people were pro or anti, hostile or friendly—that my value was not being a communicator or a speaker, or even in what I could do for him, but just that I was a person whom he loved very, very much.

"Along with the Scriptures that mean so much to me, the Lord has used my wife, Jeanie, to affirm me and to encourage me through periods of doubt, conflict, and questions I've faced, as we all certainly do from time to time."

The Ford family through the years grew to include three children—daughter Deb and sons Sandy and Kevin. How does an internationally known evangelist who spends about 40 percent of his time away from his family view the relationship he has established with his children?

Leighton Ford supplies the answer: "If the children don't see Christ lived out in us, they are not going to really listen to what we have to say.

"The Bible gives clear-cut instruction. Deuteronomy 6 talks about walking the talk and talking the walk. We as parents are to pass on to our children what we believe, and we do that by talking about these things. I like the way *The Living Bible* describes it: 'When you're out for a walk, when you go to bed, when you get up in the morning, everything you do.' I don't think that means preaching to our children so much as it means letting what we say about Christ grow naturally out of everyday life."

Prayer time in the Ford household has always been of special significance. "Our children have always seemed to open up to us more around bedtime," Jean Ford explains. "So we've had some wonderful one-to-one times together where real business gets done as we talk things out and then pray about them."

How does evangelist Leighton Ford view the church, evangelism, and world missions today? "My life has been given to world evangelism. God has given me a sense of world concern and vision beyond what I've ever had before . . . since my association with the International Congress on World

Evangelization at Lausanne, for which I have served as the chairman of the program committee." Now, once again Dr. Leighton Ford is chairman of the Lausanne committee on world evangelization. This comprises a group of about forty-seven world leaders, men, women, and young people from all over the world.

Does Leighton Ford see prophesy being fulfilled today? "Yes, I do," he affirmed, "in terms of world evangelization especially. I think we see it in Israel. One of the things that we often forget, however, is that Jesus said, 'This Gospel of the Kingdom shall be proclaimed in all the world as a testimony to all nations and then shall the end come.'

"In other words, the return of Christ is closely connected with our partnership with God in preaching and proclaiming and living this Gospel of the Kingdom in every area of the world. Now we do not expect to see the whole world converted or Christianized, but we do expect to see the Gospel make an impact among all the peoples in every area of the world. And to me one of the most exciting things is to be a part of what God is doing.

"This was not a command that Jesus gave; this was a promise. Remember, he said, 'This Gospel *shall* be proclaimed.'

"Through the Lausanne Congress it was so exciting to see the big picture, as my friend, the late Paul Little, used to say—the big picture of what God is doing. To see how, for instance, in Africa today the Christian church is growing at from two to four times the rate of population explosion, depending on what part of Africa you are in. One tribe in Ethiopia shuts down their worship services one Sunday in the month and they all go out to witness about Christ. In the last year alone 24,000 people have professed faith in Christ in that one tribe in Ethiopia alone.

"In much of Asia the church is growing at three times the rate of population explosion, in Latin America at about the same rate. But in Europe the growth of the evangelical church is almost extinct in some areas. It is almost a fossil from the past, but the Bible is 'in' and there is a fascination with the Bible and with the person of Jesus.

"Here in America, in spite of Watergate and the cynicism that exists, the growth of the playboy philosophy, and all of this, there is still a search for basic reality. There is a search on for a new moral basis, a search for spiritual reality. Materialism has not satisfied, technology is tending to scare people, and they are looking for something. We see it in the movement among athletes, for instance, in the search of young people for Christ; we see it in Bible classes springing up all across the country. The response to the crusades and to radio and television indicates to us that one of the great spiritual awakenings is having its beginnings in America today.

"But still, of this world's population of four billion, there are still nearly three billion for whom becoming a Christian is not yet a live option; some of these are unreached tribes. The Bible translators are going to some of them, but many of them are in the great cities, there is a large bulk of them in the Moslem world, in the Hindu world, the Buddhist world and in the Communist world.

"I believe with all my heart that God is opening doors today, that the Gospel shall be preached in all the world, and to that end I want to dedicate my life—all that I have, my prayers, my energy, my thoughts and my ministry—to be part of seeing God's great purpose for the ages being fulfilled, the Gospel being preached, the Church being established throughout the entire world as we look for the day when God's Kingdom shall come."

Dr. Billy Graham could not possibly have known back in January 1949 that the words he spoke to Leighton Ford, who was to become his brother-in-law as well as his associate evangelist, were to prove prophetic: "Leighton, God has given you a burden. And God always blesses the man with a burden." God has indeed blessed that man with the burden to help change the world for Christ; and the world is a better place because of him, his vision, and the dedication he exhibits with such passionate urgency.

Ed and Joyce Johnson

4
Following God's Long-Range Plan

BUSINESSMAN
EDWARD JOHNSON

BUSINESSMAN AT THE CROSSROADS

"Until we really suffer, we can never feel the beat of the heart of Christ . . . God brings us to himself over many different roads. For my part, I traveled the road of pain," writes Dale Evans Rogers in *My Spiritual Diary* (pages 9, 10). "I never knew my Saviour until I came to my life's deepest pit." She is speaking of what many have come to call their crossroads experience.

The crossroads experience is a familiar one to many. For Ed Johnson and his wife, Joyce, it came with the death of a much-loved daughter.

"Some people become bitter, some are drawn closer to the Lord. Our experience has been that we have drawn closer to God," says Johnson. "Now I am often asked to write people who are faced with crisis situations, or I am asked to speak to them, and I can confidently say, 'You are at a crossroads. You can either become bitter and blame God for this, or you can become better and allow him to use this in your life, to trust him, and move on with him. God does not blunder in sending death or other heartbreaking and difficult problems. It isn't what we think is right, it's what he knows is right for us. We may not understand God's will and his ways of working, but he is not asking for our understanding. He does want our obedience, and that involves trusting him even when the way ahead seems so dark.' "

The way seemed very dark indeed to Ed Johnson and his wife in June 1959 when word reached them that their daughter, Karen, had been killed in a three-car head-on collision on Highway 111 at the edge of the desert resort city of Palm Springs, California.

It wasn't the first time, nor was it to be the last time, that God used such a tragedy to break into the routine of busy people's lives, to jar them into a recognition of his sovereignty, the fact that he is still in control. "I know that I am better equipped now to give a point of view and to help others who are experiencing heartache than I ever was before," the distinguished-looking, white-haired Johnson says from his beautifully appointed suite of offices towering above the skyline of the City of the Angels.

Today Johnson is president and chairman of Financial Federation, Inc., a billion-dollar corporation listed on the New York Stock Exchange. But in spite of the fact that this is one of the nation's ten largest savings and loan organizations, Edward L. Johnson is a man capable of the same degree of emotional hurt as you or I. Despite his position of prominence in the investment and financial world and his knowledge and unique capabilities he is just as vulnerable to cry out and question "Why, God? Why?" as anyone else. There is no security nor comfort to be found in one's assets and investments when your dearly loved daughter's life is suddenly snuffed out in a senseless auto accident. But Johnson and his wife did not lunge out with bitter questioning, complaining against God. Many years of living close to the Lord through studying the Bible preceded this event. Now they had resources at their disposal that would carry them through the hours of heartache, longing, and grief.

At the time of Karen's death, Johnson was executive vice president, managing officer, and director of the American Savings and Loan Association in Whittier, California. Up until that time he had served in various executive capacities, a brilliant man whose horizon seemed unclouded as he rose to the top.

He had a lovely wife and five beautiful children. Their life-style was all that one could ask for. Daughter Karen was interested in sports and enjoyed riding her horse. But she was also a deeply committed Christian girl, a "campaigner for Christian causes," as *Spirit Magazine* stated it (April 1964, page 12), a radiantly enthusiastic young person who loved the church; and she was a devoted and warm friend. *Power* magazine (July, August, September 1960, pages 7–8), in writing of her, called her a priceless pearl, the name her classmates had captioned her portrait in the school annual. Those who knew her best agreed. That she was magnificently alive in Jesus Christ was known and easily recognizable.

Karen Johnson was within a few days of high school graduation and making plans to attend the University of California when she was killed instantly in an accident that claimed the lives of three other young people as well. But what makes Karen's story unusual is the fact that shortly before her death she had written and submitted a paper for a school assignment at San Marino High School. The paper was completed on Thursday night, June 4, and presented to her teacher on Friday, June 5. The next day she was in the presence of the One about whom she wrote so movingly. The paper was:

My Philosophy of Life

My philosophy of life is based on the Holy Bible and the God who wrote it. I know that he has a plan for my life and through daily prayer and reading of his Word I will be able to see it. As far as my life work or life partner, I am leaving it in his hands and am willing to do anything he says.

I feel that this philosophy is very practical and can be applied to everyday life. Every decision can be taken to the Lord in prayer and the peace that comes from knowing Jesus Christ as personal Saviour is something many cannot understand. Many search for a purpose and reason for life. I know that I am on this earth to have fellowship with God and to win others to the saving knowledge of his Son, Jesus Christ. I know that after death I will go to be with him forever.

Jesus Christ teaches love and respect for everyone throughout the New Testament, and we are not to judge anyone because he will on the judgment day. In God's sight no one person is worth any more than another.

Knowing and loving Jesus Christ personally makes me want to please him and accomplish things for his glory. Paul says in the New Testament, "Whatsoever ye do, do all to the glory of God," and "For me to live is Christ, and to die is gain."

This philosophy contains all of the seven points given in your lecture of April 20th. As I stated in the beginning:

(1) It is very practical to have someone to turn to for any decision or problem, small or large.

(2) What could be more optimistic than knowing that God has a purpose and plan for one's life and is willing to keep in constant fellowship with anyone who will. To know I have accepted Jesus Christ's gift of

salvation and will have eternal life in heaven is a most wonderful thing and brings peace to my heart. God has the best for us and if we let him he will improve our lives and solve our problems.

(3) God in his Holy Word teaches us to have love and burden for every person as Jesus Christ himself.

(4) One of my main purposes in life is to share this experience I have had with Christ and to show them the peace and happiness that it brings.

(5) This is an important goal in itself, but more completely, my aim in life is to accomplish what the Lord has for me to do, which is certainly the most worthwhile goal in life.

(6) The closer I grow to him the more happiness I find and the busier I am. He has things for me that the world could never offer, and I learn to appreciate more and more how fortunate I am.

(7) God's standards are higher than anything attainable and present a great challenge and make me realize how futile it would be for me to do the best I could, because I, being human, could never reach God's standards, and therefore never be worthy of entering heaven. God has given me contact with the best: in his world, in my born-again friends, and in my fellowship with Jesus Christ. It is well known that the highest beauty, truth, justice, and goodness is found in God's Word.

This is my philosophy, and yet it is not mine, but I am God's, and whatever I have is his and I have faith that he is the only answer and I do love him so.

Following Karen's death, her parents had the message reprinted in the hope that it would have meaning to teenagers and others who seek to make an honest appraisal of life. Entitled "A Teen-age Triumph," the paper has been published in Spanish, Swedish, Portuguese, Korean, Chinese, Russian, Japanese, and in Braille. Thousands of copies have filtered into the nooks and crannies of high schools all over the globe, and into business enterprises, homes, and churches.

"God gives you help and answers to life's questions when you need it," Johnson asserts. "When someone comes up to me and questions, 'Why did God take my baby?' and I look at them, all tied up in knots and bitter and so unhappy, I can say to them, 'Are you worried about your baby or yourself?' Then I move right in and remind them that Jesus himself said, 'Let the children come to me, for the Kingdom of God belongs to such as these.'

"I can, on the basis of Scripture, assure the parents that the baby is in his beautiful hands. 'Your baby has accomplished what you and I have not accomplished,' I tell them. 'She is in the presence of the Lord.' " Johnson is listened to and respected because people know he's been there, he's faced that crossroads experience, and they see what walking on with the Lord has done for him.

Immediately after his daughter's death, Johnson was confronted with the death of the vice president of one of the financial institutions with which he was affiliated. There was no time for excessive mourning over his own loss. At once he was on his way to comfort the grieving family, to share with them the comfort the Bible speaks of: "Blessed be God, even the Father of our Lord Jesus Christ, the Father of mercies, and the God of all comfort; Who comforteth us in all our tribulation, that we may be able to comfort them which are in any trouble, by the comfort wherewith we ourselves are comforted of God. For as the sufferings of Christ abound in us, so our consolation also aboundeth by Christ" (2 Cor. 1:3,4).

This the Johnsons were experiencing; and out of their experience there arose multiple opportunities to console others, and, in many instances, to lead others to Christ. This has continued through the years.

Someone will say to Ed Johnson: "Didn't it bother you, the accident and all? I mean, to lose a beautiful daughter in such a senseless highway accident . . ." and Johnson quickly replies, "Bother me? Why sure! It cut us up, in a sense, but we have accepted the fact that often God's ways are not necessarily our ways." Then he will pull a business card from his pocket, quickly add his home phone number, hand it to the inquirer and say, "Look, I give you this card with twenty-four-hour service. You can call me any hour around the clock if you feel you need a friend to discuss the spiritual side of this question. I'm available to you and your need. But more important, God is available."

Ed Johnson finds himself visiting terminal cancer victims in hospitals, and then later attending the memorial services for those to whom he has been able to minister words of comfort and hope, pointing them to the Savior. "The Lord gives wisdom in each situation," he says with the modesty and humility one would expect from a man of such stature, who knows full well the meaning of pain.

"I may go out on the freeway after leaving here," he will say at the bedside of a dying man, "but who knows whether I'll even get home myself or not." Then he tells of his daughter's fatal accident. "I'm reminded of the day my daughter died in a collision. I saw her a few hours before she was gone, but it was wonderful to know that she had shown her faith in Jesus Christ in such a way that it eased the burden and sorrow for us.

"Now, I feel, if that should happen to me, I would hope that you would remember too that I was trusting the Lord— trusting Jesus. I believe he completed the whole transaction—God coming in the flesh as a baby, living here upon earth, coming to manhood, living in such a way as to show us the Way to the Father, and then submitting to death for us, and rising again, and going back to heaven to be with God—he did it all for us, and the unfinished business is with us." Johnson pauses and explains, "This is one of the ways God has enabled me to use the experience of Karen's death to reach others for him. As I talk to an individual, I show him how he can reach out to God and receive Christ into his heart."

Ed Johnson has seen many a weak hand reach out to take his as he leads them in prayer. "I can't take a man's temperature on a spiritual deal," he says, "but I've had people tell me that a loved one with whom I'd prayed had no trouble dying. Why? Because they were ready to face God.

"What does it take to become a Christian? God uses Christ's blood and our faith and saves us. The Apostle Paul put it like this: 'For God sent Christ Jesus to take the punishment for our sins and to end all God's anger against us. He used Christ's blood and our faith as the means of saving us from his wrath. In this way he was being entirely fair . . . And now in these days he can receive sinners in this same way, because Jesus took away their sins' (Rom. 3:25, 26).

"We need to remember, however, that God's not going to save us unless we supply our part. The faith element bridges the gap for everybody who can't fully understand what it's all about. The Bible makes it very clear that when we 'believe on the Lord Jesus Christ we shall be saved' (Acts 16:31). Such believing is indicative of faith."

Not only have events in recent years brought Ed Johnson into contact with the terminally ill and the bereaved, but with those in public office. Unhesitatingly, he will tell such a person that he is praying for him. It is more than a "dear God, bless those in public office"; it is remembering them individually by name, and the peculiar responsibilities that have been thrust upon them.

"When we are dealing politically, we stand up in our political thrust," Johnson explains. "Why not stand up and be counted as Christians?

"Christ was nonpartisan. His way of salvation fits Republicans, Democrats, independents, blacks, whites, yellows, reds, rich and poor, educated and uneducated. I dare anybody to come up with any kind of imaginative program that does what Christianity does. God had equal rights long before we started campaigning for them."

In the magnificent suite of offices on the upper floor of Financial Federation in downtown Los Angeles, Ed Johnson has installed a reverse screen. Films can be shown from the rear and those viewing the film see a life-size screen picture. The day I was invited to a beautiful buffet in the offices, Mr. Johnson had a prestigious group of men and women in.

He takes films such as *His Land*, produced by the Billy Graham Evangelistic Association and World Wide Pictures, to dinners at the Century Plaza and elsewhere, many of which he hosts for dignitaries that frequently honor overseas ambassadors and their retinues, or for other groups. When he speaks at such a function he might preface his remarks, for instance, with comments such as this: "This is a day when we should have clear identification, sometimes in business parlance called full disclosure. I want to tell you tonight that I'm a Christian."

Mr. Johnson looked at me with a twinkle in his eye and commented, "After saying that recently at a function largely attended by some of my Jewish friends and acquaintances, including the Ambassador from Israel, I remember saying to myself and to the Lord, 'Did I just say that? Oh, Lord, that must have been your idea, not mine.' But that night the whole house broke out with applause. I went on to tell the audience, 'The picture you are about to see is an evidence of Christian love for the people of Israel. It's one way that Dr.

Billy Graham has been able to show his love, and the love of other Christians, for Jewish people. And what I think will particularly impress you is that here is a documentary of the great miracle of Israel, filmed by a Christian studio right here in nearby Burbank.'

"To show that picture diagonally across that big ballroom at the Century Plaza took a lot of doing. Afterwards the comments were remarkable, to say the least. Only the Lord knows what actually happened in the hearts of many of those who were watching."

Ed Johnson is a very practical man with keen insights. "Sometimes in our zeal for the Lord we get the emphasis where it doesn't belong, and people start looking at us instead of Christ. There is danger in that, and I am not unaware of it. Often when I talk, to teenagers especially, this will happen. I will have with me the little reprint which has Karen's picture on the front, and kids will say, 'Oh, what a beautiful girl she was.' And I must remind them, 'Now I don't want your eyes on Karen. I want you to focus your attention on the most important thing she left for you and said in that school assignment—her identification with Christ. She didn't mention her mother or her father. She could have at least said something nice about her mother, even if she wanted to skip her father. But she didn't. And she didn't say what church she belonged to. What she said, I believe, was deeply inspired within her.' "

Johnson paused, deep in reflection, leaning forward, hands cupped together, and with emphasis said, "If what we say for the Lord is, in fact, inspired, then the message we are trying to communicate for him will be there, and we as individuals will be phased out in the hearer's thinking."

How does the Bible relate to this businessman's thinking? "I accept the Bible totally as the Word of God. That's very fundamental with me, and rarely will I speak without mentioning the fact that the Bible is like a benchmark. Some of your readers may not know what a benchmark is. A benchmark is a surveyor's mark made on a permanent landmark that has a known position and altitude. It is generally a bronze plug used as a reference point in determining other altitudes within a given line of levels.

"When they built the towers next door to this building, they had to know that they were on the right lot. So you start at a benchmark, and you move. Incidentally, George Washington started the survey system in the United States. There are intermediary benchmarks—the government has established across the country principle ones in each area. So when they build a building, the engineers refer to the benchmark book. They find one and then say, now we'll go from here. Then they will find another one and check it out.

"So the Bible is my benchmark. I have no problem with the Scriptures. Absolutely none. That's where faith comes in. I don't have to prove everything, and I am not so presumptuous as to think that I am supposed to totally understand the complete writings of God Almighty.

"My starting point is the Bible, and I never veer from it. When an individual, or a religious training institution such as a seminary or Bible College, leaves the benchmark, then they are in trouble.

"I remember the time I talked to a Pan Am pilot deadheading it back to Los Angeles. He had his flight manual in his lap. I said to him, 'Well, captain, I see you have your flight manual. I have one too.'

"He said to me, 'Are you a flyer?'

"I answered back, 'Well in a fashion. I'm going through this world on wings.' Then I gave him the message about God's love in sending Christ. When I was all through, I said, 'Give me your card and I'll mail you a copy of my flight manual when we get back.' And I did. I sent him a copy of *Good News For Modern Man: The New Testament in Today's English Version.*

"Another time I was flying across the country next to a fellow who was reading a paperback. I had *Good News for Modern Man* with me, and we started talking. After I shared with him the message of Christ, he said, 'How come you know all these things and I don't?'

"The tendency among so many people, I have discovered, is to delegate all spiritual teaching to their church, their priest, minister, or somebody else. They do not read, study and search the Scriptures for themselves as the Apostle Paul tells us we are to do: 'Study to show thyself approved unto God, a workman that needeth not to be ashamed, rightly dividing the word of truth' (2 Tim. 2:15).

"That day on the plane I answered the gentleman's question by saying, 'It's a personal relationship to God through Christ that counts, and we learn about that from his written Word to us—I like to read it from this paperback version,' and I handed him my copy of *Good News For Modern Man*.

"I looked at his paperback and said, 'You've got a paperback there. It's just a question of which book you want to read and spend the most time in.' I offered him my paperback to keep, and he accepted it gladly."

Johnson looked at me intently. "It's another example of the availability of the Gospel to us, particularly in this country. And yet people steer around it and away from it, and don't want to face up to reality. They just hope somebody else is handling the matter for them and that when it comes time to die the whole transaction will have been taken care of for them without any effort on their part.

"I believe that my part in God's program is to dispel such false notions and wrong thinking. God made us as individuals and we're not locked into a pattern. He has given us freedom of choice. And that's great. It's personal. That's what it's all about.

"In my business I deal with long-range planning. We believe people are foolish who do not take into account their future and its needs. We try to help them invest wisely. We are totally committed to the business of promoting personal thrift and the long-range benefits that will thus accrue to them. Therefore, a realistic businessman will look at life in its totality.

"How do I relate this to my own relationship with the Lord? It is either God's plan or my own. The Word of God assures me that his plan is far better than anything I could possibly devise. The importance of long-range planning—thinking in terms of my present commitment to Christ and what this will mean for all eternity—is very important, for I live out my life in a relationship with him that can have an influence in the lives of others. I trust that in some small way I am helping to change the world for him."

Just as Edward and Joyce Johnson's daughter, Karen, found the Christian life exciting, so can the reader. Karen walked with God joyously and exuberantly: Her brief life was a triumphant testimony to the reality of life in Christ. In the same way, her parents see all of life in the perspective of one's relationship to God through his provision for us in Christ who is our access to the Father.

Ed Johnson—businessman, financier, father, husband, friend, and committed Christian—says, "I sincerely recommend that the reader study what God has to offer. Begin with his benchmark, the Bible. I believe you will find no other plan for investment of one's life that offers a combination of such high returns in the here and now, and assured security for the future."

Bishop Festo Kivengere

5
Africa's Gift to the Church

EVANGELIST
FESTO KIVENGERE

His little brothers and sisters sat out on the hillside crying, and he brushed the tears away from his eyes, too. Ten-year-old boys don't like to be seen crying, but Festo Kivengere found it just as difficult as his younger brothers and sisters to keep the tears from falling as he read about Jesus dying on the cross. He had learned to read in just three months from the African evangelist who came to the village to preach and teach. His first primer was the Bible Gospel of Luke. As they stumbled over the words, the meaning touched something deep within the hearts of these children. "It was the story of the crucifixion that got to us," Festo explains. "What made sense about the story was how much this man Jesus loved." Eagerly the children crowded around their brother as he took time out from cattle-herding to learn to read. Festo became their teacher.

That was many years ago. Today Festo Kivengere—teacher, evangelist, bishop, brother—is called by many the outstanding black evangelist in Africa, with a ministry that takes him around the world. Missionary statesmen, such as Dr. Paul S. Rees of World Vision International, speak of him as being "under God, Africa's gift to the church universal." How it all began is an amazing story of the Holy Spirit at work in the heart of a man destined to be used to help change the world for Christ.

Festo's first encounter with the Bible was when he saw peculiar-looking marks on paper spring to life with meaning in the story of a man named Jesus. Festo, however, did not realize the claim Christ was going to make upon his life, for while the story brought quick tears to his eyes, he was bound by the superstitious Bantu worship which formed such an important part of the culture of his tribe.

One year later the young Ugandan enrolled in a mission school. He must have wanted to learn very badly, for it is difficult to imagine an eleven-year-old willingly rising very early each morning in order to make the ten-mile hike to school.

"I was born into a non-Christian family in Kigezi, Western Uganda," he explains. "My father was a keen worshipper of the gods of our tribe. I, as the first-born, was early initiated into the mysteries of this worship. Devout as my father was, he never seemed to me to have found that after which he was so keenly searching. I was about nine years old when this observation first struck me."

Bantu worship imposed upon the people stringent rules, and the taboos of the spirits held the people in the grip of superstition and fears.

With his head Festo received the teachings at the mission school, but for five more years his young heart remained empty, his life unchanged. By now Festo was attending a high school boarding school. "It was 1936 when the wind began to blow. What happens when God's love is poured into our hearts by the Holy Spirit? The Apostle Paul, the well-trained ex-bigot, tells us about it in Romans 5:1–5. I know something about this from experience. Men are absolutely liberated with another power that is beyond any power of their own.

"A breath of life began to sweep through the valley of dry bones, even as Ezekiel the prophet prophesied," Festo says. "Our school and church was like that valley described in the Old Testament, and we were like dry bones spiritually.

"But God, because he is the God of life and love, started moving. Some men with shining faces came to hold meetings, but only two people came to Christ. The truth, however, went deep. It was like a time bomb. About three months later the real impact of the meetings began to be felt. They had taught us a lovely chorus, *Spirit of the Living God, fall afresh on me,* which we sang in our mother tongue again and again, and then the breath began to come.

"People could not sleep in our town. God's Holy Spirit was too close. In our school dormitories, boys did not sleep. They woke up weeping and started praying. Hearing them pray you became shaken, and one after another of us began to find God. I myself was gripped with conviction. There was a desperate need in my heart, and hearing these boys praying and talking about Jesus, accentuated my need and I heard myself crying out for Christ. I fell to my knees and accepted him into my heart.

"Then people began dreaming dreams and seeing visions of heaven and hell. People would walk into our community from as far away as twenty miles to tell what they saw in a dream. I remember seeing a man being led by the hand. He had been blinded—by the same light as St. Paul saw—and he had to be led by the hand to give his testimony to the church."

Plainly, this was revival. Festo's memories of that movement in 1936 in Western Uganda are very vivid. "Things began to happen rapidly after that. Conviction of sin came upon people. The Word of God became real and alive. The church was packed and the atmosphere was charged with the power of the Spirit."

But what were the visible results of all of this? Festo is quick to tell. "People were rejoicing and talking from experience and singing praises to God. Jesus was so close, they talked about him while shopping. They talked about him when they drew water. People were even converted at the watering places for cattle—cattlemen speaking to cattlemen. It was wonderful! This was like what happened in the New Testament.

"But if you did not like it, it was a very frightening experience." As was to be expected in such a situation, there were those who tried to stop the movement and work of the Holy Spirit. One such person was Festo's uncle, the chief. "He was a good chief, a big man over six feet tall, and a very respected, church-going gentleman. He told his people to make these Christians stop. 'If they tell you about Jesus,' he said, 'beat them up.'

"Many of them were badly beaten. I remember one man who beat up a Christian who had given his testimony, but when this man went home, he couldn't sleep that night. He woke up under conviction and was wonderfully saved and came back to my uncle, the chief. This so alarmed my uncle that he issued the warning to be careful and the order not to beat Christians any more for fear too many would be converted."

Certainly it was New Testament Christianity springing to life in Uganda, a repeat of the Book of Acts in the twentieth century. The Christians could not be stopped.

Festo's conversion experience was real, but in his words, "I became worldly and backslid. I was in the wilderness for awhile. The convicting inner voice never left me, but I tried

to drown it out with drinking, smoking, and doing everything possible to get away." He didn't want "Churchianity,"
nor did he want to go back to his father's religion. The battle
with the enemy was a struggle.

The Apostle Paul speaks of the devil like this: "For we
wrestle not against flesh and blood, but against prin-
cipalities, against powers, against the rulers of the darkness
of this world, against spiritual wickedness in high places"
(Eph. 6:12). Festo was wrestling. Satan threw every strategy
and trick at him, knowing that if he lost this young black
man he was losing a real prize.

The life or death struggle continued, with nineteen-year-
old Festo fighting to resist the tug of the Holy Spirit.

Emptiness. Meaningless. That's what life was to the young
man who all through school had showed such promise. "But
God is a wonderful strategist," he says today. "God had so
planned my life that when I finished my training as a teacher,
I was posted to teach in my former first school in my own
village."

The year was 1940. Revival had spread from village to
village. "As I look back now, I realize anew that what was
happening was just tremendous—hundreds were being saved
each week. Everywhere people were making restitution to
those they had wronged; murderers were repenting of having
killed people; others were going to the government offices
and paying taxes they had evaded for years. People were
even returning cows they had stolen ten years before. And
there I was in the midst of it all."

Festo's mentality up to this point had been that of an ag-
nostic—he refused to fully believe in God because God is not
provable. God is too big for a test tube. Festo's life was like a
spinning top,as he describes it. It was hollow and direc-
tionless. How many there are racing through life like that.
The underlying philosophy, of course, is that if a person is

moving swiftly enough, he can't be stopped to philosophize about sin, sorrow or death. But inside is that gnawing fear that all is not well.

All was not well for Festo on a Sunday afternoon in October of 1941, when he was coming home from a drinking party. "I hated to hear about peace and joy when I was miserable, so instead of going to church, I spent my Sundays drinking. I couldn't love my neighbor when I couldn't even love myself at times.

"I was cycling madly along the road with drink in my head, when I was stopped by a young teacher friend of mine. We taught in the same school, and we had had a few escapades together.

"He looked me full in the face and said, 'Festo, a few hours ago Jesus Christ became a living reality to me. And I know he is in my heart right now.'

"That fellow had never spoken like that before. Then he went on, 'I want to say good-bye to you, my dear friend, and to apologize for the sort of thing we have shared and for what we said against God. Festo, I shall never live like that again. Now I belong to Jesus.'

"He left me and went on. I tried to ride my bicycle, but I felt like a shadow. Instantly I saw that friend of mine had the reality I had missed all the while."

Festo arrived at his house with a funny feeling inside that stirred him to action. The same kind of tears that had streamed down his face long years before out on the hillside when he first read about Christ's crucifixion now freely flowed once again as he knelt by his bed, crying out, "God, if you are there, and if Christ actually died for sinners like me, if you can do something about me, then do it! If the Bible is not a mere storybook cooked up by Europeans to deceive us, here am I, save me."

Festo felt the burden of sin and sinful living fall off. Judgment was gone. "God broke my heart open and introduced me to the living Jesus, who entered in. I was no longer a spinning top. He gave my life the direction that was missing, and it has lasted until this very day. I know it will last for all eternity."

At this time the Ugandans were still under British rule as a protectorate. "I had a lot of hang-ups with some of the English people, missionaries and all," Festo confesses. "In particular there was one who was in education and under whom I worked. I hated that man, I don't know why. One day I knew Christ was saying to me, 'You hate that man and yet he is your brother.' That was a revolutionary word: brother! He was English and he was a white man. But I knew that Jesus was saying, 'I love that man just as much as I love you, and I tell you that he is your brother. Now go to him.'

"I found myself saying, 'But Lord, what shall I say to him?'

"And God told me to go and tell him I was sorry that I had hated him and to ask his forgiveness. When I came to that man's house, I walked in and embraced him and explained what Christ had done for me. 'Jesus' love has shown me that you are my brother,' I said to him. Do you know that we wept in each others' arms! I had bicycled fifty miles through the mountains under the tropical sun to a white man whom I had hated, but I felt as if my bicycle had an engine! My world had changed; now I had a brother in that house, not a lonely Englishman whom I hated. Such is the power of Christ. So far as I am concerned, the only real power I know is the power of Christ, and him on the cross. Through his sacrificial love, power is released to meet broken men and women, broken by hatred, fear, suspicion, tyranny and oppression, and change them into friends, brothers and sisters."

Festo continued to teach high school in his hometown, Kabale, Uganda, and in 1942 married Mera, whom he had known all his life. Mera, too, came to know Christ through the revival. "God was blessing us," he says, "and men and women who were brought into the liberty of Christ were in the grip of a tremendous burden of love to share the Christ who had done so much for them. We were part of these. We would go out in groups of four or five, from valley to valley, spending weekends in churches or wherever we could gather people together who would listen. Uganda was covered in a matter of about five years by these evangelistic teams who were passing the good news on, and the country was evangelized in this way. But it was all the work of the fire of the Holy Spirit as it broke through to individual hearts.

"Soon there was an even wider breakthrough as the Word spread into Kenya, Tanzania, Ruanda, Burundi, and some parts of eastern Congo. The Spirit crossed denominational barriers."

Festo and Mera taught for five years in the schools of Uganda and then felt the call of the Lord to go to Tanzania as missionaries. For the next thirteen years they worked there, facing strong resistance at first. "Our testimony was opposed."

In his own unique way, Festo dramatizes his story, confessing even to spiritual pride, which is ruinous to the work of Christ. "As soon as you become judgmental," he says, "you become as cold as ice. You can't judge and love at the same time. You become dryer and more puzzled. God said to us, 'You are suffering from the sins of success. You came from an area where things were comparatively easy—meetings were warm, people were being saved. You are acting as if you were still there. You have to learn a new lesson. You cannot feed on past experiences. You must rest on me, rely on me as the one who can satisfy, direct, and help you to love.'

"And so we had to repent. We did not repent of our testimony, but we did repent of our holier-than-thou attitude.

Then God began to liberate us quietly and help us. Then we began loving like Jesus.

"You must be liberated from the wrong spirit before you can pray and expect the Holy Spirit to work through you," he explains. "As we received the touch of Jesus' love and mercy, we were able to pray, 'Master, touch where you wish, for yours is a hand of love.' "

Then it was that God broke through into the Wagogo tribe of central Tanganyika (as it was called at that time), and this moving of God's Spirit has since become a notable part of the phenomenon of missions in Africa.

It was in 1959 that Festo Kivengere's worldwide ministry began with a preaching tour through Australia. Then in 1960 he was asked to travel through East Africa interpreting for Dr. Billy Graham. By this time the Kivengere family had grown to include four daughters, Peace, Joy, Hope and Charity. And Festo's vision for world evangelism had also grown. He had caught the vision of sharing Christ and was drawn into becoming a full-time evangelist.

In the fall of 1960 Billy Graham invited Festo to share with thirty-five international evangelists holding a conference in Switzerland to assess their effectiveness in the light of the world crises. God used him to touch the lives and ministries of these men when he shared his secret of a simple walk with Christ.

Since then, Festo's ministry in evangelistic crusades, conventions, and conferences has taken him to many countries of Africa and Europe as well as America, Canada, Israel, Australia, New Zealand, the South Sea Islands, Japan, China, Russia, and parts of Asia. Wherever he goes, there is a fresh testimony to the grace of God.

In the midst of all his busy evangelistic crusade activity, he took time out to study in the United States at the Pittsburgh Theological Seminary where he earned a Bachelor of Divinity degree. Near the close of his training there, he was ordained by the Episcopal Diocese of Pittsburgh. Later, in Uganda, he was ordained priest without a parish in the Church of Uganda. Still later, in 1972, Festo was unanimously called by the Kigezi Diocese to be its bishop. This ended years of tribal struggle during which the Christians were unable to agree on an African bishop. There was unanimous consent by the other bishops of Uganda, and Festo was consecrated that year, with the understanding that his worldwide ministry would not be cut off.

It was in 1968 at the West African Congress on Evangelism that Festo met Michael Cassidy, the young founder and leader of the African Enterprise evangelistic team that God was using in South Africa in a notable way. Festo found a warm unity in Michael and a oneness of vision. Festo's interest and association with African Enterprise work continues to this day as he and the other evangelists dedicate themselves to world change by spiritual awakening. These evangelists serve not only their own countries and East Africa, but also all the independent nations of black Africa, and they respond to calls from beyond the continent.

Festo Kivengere has discovered that "to be alive in Christ is the greatest thing in the world."

"Jesus is all love for the unlovely. Jesus is all fullness for the empty. Jesus is all perfection for the imperfect. Jesus is all healing for the sick. All you need to do is to say to the Holy Spirit, 'Oh, blessed Enlightener, just open my blind eyes!'

"This was the excitement of St. Paul when he said, 'I am crucified with Christ' (Gal. 2:20). Apart from Christ, I am dead and finished. With Christ, I am vibrating with life. But the life that I live is not mine. It is the life of Christ in and through me.

"A saint is one who has learned that there is *nothing* in

him, and that *all* is in Christ for him. He has learned to embrace Christ for every moment, in every aspect of his life.

"Yes, to be alive in Christ is the greatest thing in the world!"

Fern Lindquist

Rex Lindquist

6
Channels Only

BOOKSELLERS
REX AND FERN LINDQUIST

In 1896, prospectors discovered gold in the Klondike region of the Yukon Territory, just across the border from Alaska. In 1897, Seattle newspaper headlines screamed out the words "A Ton of Gold." Subsequently, thousands of gold seekers boarded any craft that would float and headed for the great northland of Alaska in search of a share in the pot of gold. Some, indeed, discovered gold and riches beyond their imaginations; others found romance and adventure; still others were doomed to disappointment, disillusionment and even death. Rex and Fern Lindquist, too, went to Alaska to discover gold—not of monetary value, but of eternal priceless worth.

"The enchanting forty-ninth state was our home for thirteen years," the gracious Fern Lindquist related. "Truly it was enchanting in its immense size, its incredible beauty, its fantastic wealth of oil, minerals, natural gas and its vast forests." The Lindquists were overawed by the grandeur of this giant of the fifty states comprising the Union. They discovered it to be an outdoorsmen's paradise—an untamed wilderness attracting expert mountain climbers who could tackle some of the highest peaks in North America, sports-

men who could stalk enormous brown bears and swift cari-
bou, and fishermen who could battle record-size salmon and
trout. Like many early Americans who thought of Alaska as
a region of worthless waste of ice and snow, they were in for
some surprises.

"The name Alaska comes from an Aleutian word meaning
great land," Fern Lindquist explained, "and we found it to be
so, not just because of its fantastic beauty and valuable natural resources but because of its people." People, then, were
what drew the Lindquists to Alaska in search of incalculable
treasure.

Very early in their lives Rex and Fern discovered that God
works through human channels to change the course of the
world and the destinies of people. "The Book of Acts in the
New Testament wouldn't make thrilling reading if it were
confined to the story of early church finance," Rex explains,
"but it is the work of the Holy Spirit through human channels that thrills the reader with God's mercy, love, and
power. The early church relied on the Holy Spirit."

Before Alaska, in the Lindquists' experience, there were the
growing-up years in Minnesota; seven years in an Omaha
pastorate; twelve years in Denver; then Alaska, "land of
superlatives," as Fern so graphically describes it in her lectures.

It wasn't until Rex Lindquist had decided to go into the
ministry as a young man that his maternal grandmother told
him, "Rex, the doctor said you wouldn't live until morning
when you were three years old. I prayed to God and said,
'Thy will be done, Lord, but if you will only let him live, I
will dedicate him to you as a preacher-boy.' " Rex survived.

Fern Hanson's grandmother played an important role in
her life also, for it was to her that Fern confided, after
meeting Rex for the first time at a church rally, "Grandma,
this is the man I'm going to marry someday." Her grandmother never forgot it and reminded her lovely granddaugh-
ter on occasion to set her goals high.

Fern was a bright student who particularly enjoyed reading about faraway places in the world and often dreamt of traveling. Little did she know that God, out of the great storehouse of his infinite wisdom, love and riches, was going to make her dreams come true.

When asked what she wanted to be when she grew up, Fern would quickly reply, "A minister's wife," to which her mother would respond, "Fern, if you were a pastor's wife, you'd operate a free hotel and restaurant." Fern's mother's prophecy has been fulfilled. Rarely have we ever seen anyone who entertains as splendidly and graciously as Fern Lindquist!

When Fern was seventeen, she slipped out of the choir loft one Sunday, and in her words, "I John 5 verse 13 became a reality in my experience. 'These things have I written unto you that believe on the name of the Son of God; that ye may know that ye have eternal life, and that ye may believe on the name of the Son of God.' "

Because Rex had been raised in a store atmosphere (his parents owned a men's clothing store and a women's millinery shop), he entertained the thought of becoming a businessman and studied towards that goal. While he could very easily have relied on his parents to put him through college, his independent nature surfaced, and he decided to earn his own way. He stayed at the Rescue Mission on Skid Row in Minneapolis, rubbing shoulders with the transients, and standing in line with them for a meal ticket ($1.50 per week). He was musically inclined and played his cornet five nights a week at the mission, in addition to using his musical background to help get a job. An early commitment, at age twelve, decided the direction his life would take, and he never veered from the course.

Fern, too, worked her way through Northwestern. As Fern and Rex found they enjoyed each other's company more and more, their relationship took a serious turn. "We prayed on every date," she says. "At first we thanked God for the good times we were having, and later we started thanking him for our relationship. I received my beautiful diamond on Valentine's Day, and we were engaged for almost two years. It was a wonderful time of getting to know each other." On September 23, 1936, they were married by Dr. Harry A. Rimmer in Duluth, Minnesota.

When Rex accepted his first call to become a minister, he wanted to show Fern the parsonage. "I had visions of a darling white bungalow, a picket fence, and roses rambling on trellises. Imagine my disappointment when we drove up to the place. I had never seen such a ramshackle building in my life. It was horribly weatherbeaten and terribly in need of paint. And the inside was even worse."

Rex looked at the house, then looked at his bride, took her in his arms and said, "Well, honey, some of our classmates are in huts in Africa."

"Material blessings may make things more comfortable, but they do not assure happiness. Rex made the immense salary of fifty dollars a month, but already then we covenanted with God that we would give two-tenths of our income to him. That left us with forty dollars to live on. But we never went hungry, the farmers were so good in bringing us food and in helping in practical ways," Fern recalled.

"Then we received a call to a pastorate in Omaha. They offered Rex eighty-five dollars a month. I received my first major lesson on stewardship there. Rex wanted to increase our giving to a third of our income. 'Honey,' I said, 'we are just making ends meet now. I don't know how we can do that.' But Rex was patiently persistent. 'The world's needs are so great,' he would remind me. Then Rex suggested we put out a fleece, like Gideon in the Bible.

" 'Lord,' we prayed, 'if you want us to increase our giving, give us a sign in the way of a personal gift within seven days.' At the time Rex had a radio program. Up to this time we hadn't received any personal gifts for this work. God really tried our faith; nothing happened until the seventh day. We received a letter and this person wanted to give us a gift of a refrigerator because we had an old-fashioned icebox. These were Depression days, and this was quite a gift!

"But there was more—there was also enough to purchase a white tabletop range to go with the new refrigerator. When we went to the appliance store to do this, the man gave us a new vacuum cleaner. After that, every time I opened the refrigerator, or cooked on that stove, or vacuumed the floor, I was reminded of how God answered that fleece; but also that I should never hinder Rex in what he wanted to give to the Lord's work.

"Shortly after that God showed us that we should give 50 percent of our income to his work."

Increasingly through the years, God put on their hearts an interest in and concern for world missions. Rex explains this leading. "The Lord led us to see that the testimony of a church can be just as practical as the testimony of a layman. And as we sought before God for direction we recognized that the only purpose and excuse for a church is 'Go ye into all the world and preach the Gospel to every creature.' That's Matthew 28:19–20. It's biblical.

"After applying to two different missionary agencies we were definitely set at rest that our call was to do something about 'the whole world,' and while we were to stay here in person we were to be his channels in sending forth the Gospel to every corner. That conviction led to the realization that the only way to fire missionary enthusiasm is to let people see a life aflame with the passion to win souls. In our Omaha church, then, we determined, with God's help, to put away sales, suppers, and other forms of commercialism or means of raising money for missions and instead to challenge the people not to lean on the arm of flesh but to trust God. We were a church of 150 members, but we set a goal of twenty fully supported missionaries in ten years' time."

Seven years later, when the Lindquists felt God calling them to a new work in Denver, Colorado, they left behind a flourishing work and a constant revival spirit. Eight missionaries had been sent out, a widely heard radio program was being broadcast, and God had proved to them that he was able "to do exceedingly abundantly above all that we ask or think."

New challenges awaited them at the Church of the Open Door in Denver. There they founded the Rocky Mountain Bible Institute (of which Rex is president emeritus today), and Rex was tremendously active in Youth for Christ work (which he had also done in Omaha). This work brought the friendship of Dr. Torrey Johnson, Dr. Billy Graham, Bob Pearce, Theodore Epp, Merv Rosell, and others.

Dr. Billy Graham dedicated their storefront church in Denver; in succeeding years they were to outgrow four buildings. Why? Rex says, "All because of our missionary emphasis. People caught a missionary vision, and there was no holding them back."

The Youth for Christ rallies consumed much of his time. It was while in Denver preparing for a rally where Torrey Johnson was to be the speaker that Rex became overfatigued. "I couldn't even attend," he said. "The Lord spoke to me: 'Rex, it's either the church or your Youth for Christ work.' We'd been there already eight years, but I felt God was telling me to continue in the pastorate."

The Bible Institute was rapidly growing. "Training centers for Christian young people are desperately needed in the world today. Isaiah 6:8 sees the prophet repeating a question the Lord asked: 'Whom shall I send, and who will go for us?' When people are given the opportunity for a Christ-centered education, the possibility is much greater that they will respond by saying, 'Here am I, Lord; send me.' "

The Open Door Children's Home came into being to provide a home for children in need. It seemed there was no end to the ideas that came to the Lindquists. But uppermost in their minds at all times was the need to send missionaries directly to the fields of the world. Not only were they doing this on an ever-expanding scale, but they were also working in close cooperation with existing independent missions wherever possible. Therefore they pledged themselves to work with such ministries as the African Inland Mission, American Inland Mission, Berean Mission, Evangelical Alliance Mission, Gospel Missionary Union, Missionary Gospel Fellowship, Rio Grande Bible Institute, and the Sudan Interior Mission.

"Our work was such," Rex relates, "that we made it possible for givers to designate directly to individuals for whom the Holy Spirit had burdened them. In turn these missionaries wrote acknowledgments directly from the field in personal notes. It was a personal touch that God greatly blessed."

The church at Omaha had given Rex and Fern, among other things, a plaque with the words of Jeremiah 33:3 engraved: "Call unto me and I will show thee great and mighty things."

For many years they had been calling to God asking for a child. Rexine, named after her daddy, was the Lindquists tenth wedding anniversary present. "We adopted her when she was a six-pound, ten-day-old baby." She was to bring another dimension of joy into their lives.

"As soon as Rexine was able to understand she would ask us to tell or read her a story. She loved Bible stories, but the story she asked for the most was, 'Tell me how you got me, mommy.' So I'd repeat over and over again how we prayed and waited for a child, but God made us wait for ten long years because he had a special baby girl that he had chosen for us. Then I'd add, 'You see, honey, some mommies and daddies have children, but some of them didn't really want them. You were wanted and chosen by us so you are special. That's why we adopted you.'

"When Rexine played with other children she'd comment, 'I wasn't just borned, I was 'dopted.'

"We were strict disciplinarians. One Sunday I sat with her

on the front pew because I was to sing a solo. She was quite restless and thought she could take advantage of me knowing it was a long way to the back. That Sunday I had to take her out three times, spank her, and carry her back in. Her will had to be broken. She always behaved well after that.

"My husband and I never disagreed before her about the discipline. This is so very important for parents," she emphasized.

"After we spanked her, she was asked to go to her room, tell Jesus she was sorry, and then tell us. Sometimes that took a long time. It's very difficult to say I'm sorry for any of us. And sometimes we ourselves had to say those very words to her.

"But after punishing her, many times I'd get on my knees and weep—I loved her and would rather have been more easy on her, but because I loved her, I knew in my heart that training requires discipline. God does the same with us."

After twelve years in Denver, once again the Lindquists found themselves thinking longingly about the mission field. The West Indies appealed to them, but there was a language problem. At their age they did not feel inclined to begin language study. "We went to the library and started studying about Alaska. The more we read and the more we studied, the more intrigued we became. It was 1956. We'd been in Denver long enough, we felt. There were twenty-three missionaries out on the field.

"But Anchorage, Alaska, was something else. We discovered in our reading and studying that out of one hundred churches, less than a dozen were self-supporting. We sold our home and furniture, bought a camper-size trailer, and drove up the Alcan Highway."

It was July 11, 1956, when the Lindquist family set out on their venture to the last frontier, so called because much of the state of Alaska is not fully settled.

In a letter written from Duluth, Minnesota, before departure, they noted that by the time they arrived in Anchorage, they would have added over five thousand miles to their station wagon, two thousand of which would be on unpaved gravel and dirt highway.

"In twenty years of pastoral ministry we have seen many go to the mission field. We have received thousands of dollars in offerings for missionaries. Often we have been burdened to go to the foreign mission field and twice we applied for service in Africa, but the Lord asked us to stay and send others.

"Now the Lord has given to us the joyous privilege of going to a needy land. We won't be preaching in a foreign language, but we shall be pastoring a church that serves as a headquarters for missionaries who do minister to the many Indians and Eskimos. We shall be also serving one of the neediest English-speaking communities in the world."

Fourteen days later they arrived in Anchorage. "We were awed by the immensity of the wilderness area of Canada, the Yukon Territory, and Alaska," Fern wrote. "We ran out of superlatives and felt completely frustrated as we realized that we could not possibly picture this trip and this country to our friends.

"Brilliant fireweed bordered the highway most of the way. As we moved northward the days grew longer. We discovered that the west would be still light at midnight and the sun would be brightly shining again at 2 A.M.

"One day we saw an unusual Indian cemetery. Neat, colorfully painted houses covered each grave. The houses were about four by six feet and from five to six feet high, complete with curtained windows. No doors on these houses. No one would want to enter and the occupants couldn't leave. Only the Christian has hope beyond the grave."

Their work was cut out for them. Twenty years before their arrival the city boasted two thousand residents. At the

time they began their work there, it was a bustling community with a civilian and military population of ninety-five thousand.

Rex wrote: "This is one of the most rapidly growing cities in North America. It is destined to become one of the busiest air centers in the world.

"Twenty firms have leased over four million acres for oil exploration. The natural resources of Alaska are an untapped treasurehouse, which will undoubtedly accelerate the population boom still further. Men have come here to make money—and they have made money their god.

"Every visitor is amazed to find a modern traffic-jammed city at the end of the Alaska highway. Your first reaction is that you just cannot believe that this is to be found in Alaska.

"It is difficult to measure the spiritual pulse of the cities of North America, but we sincerely believe that Anchorage is the neediest English-speaking city of this size on the continent."

Not wishing to solicit funds for their support, the Lindquists saw the need for and set about to establish the Alaska Bible Store, which became a ministry in itself, supplying the needs of Anchorage churches as well as mission stations in the interior.

Rex remembers so well the first visit that Kenneth Taylor, then representing the Moody Literature Department, made to his store. "Rex, you've got to move your store into town," Ken Taylor said.

Rex relates, "Ken walked the streets of Anchorage looking for a suitable location for me, so determined was he that the Alaska Bible Store should be in the city itself. He wasn't able to find a suitable place, but he did motivate me to go on looking.

"Soon thereafter I found a five-room house in downtown Anchorage, and each carpeted room became an attractive department of the store.

"This location was rented without a lease, for it was marked for removal.

"In a little over a year, notice came to vacate, but the Lord provided a beautiful store building where we could continue expansion. Each month the rent was paid. Each month the business grew, and soon we were able to invest several hundred dollars monthly into the missionary program and property development of the church.

"Nine years later the store was sold for thirty thousand dollars. By this time the church had grown to the place where it could support the pastor without retrenching a penny on the missionary and radio outreach. What a miracle!"

The Lindquists were in Alaska when it was granted statehood on June 30, 1958. "What a day of celebration that was! The headlines declared 'We're In!' As word spread through Alaska, stores closed, huge bonfires blazed, church bells pealed, and sirens wailed. Parades, parties, and festival gaiety enlivened the whole daylit night, for there is no darkness in Alaska on June 30."

Alaska has five thousand glaciers and ice fields. These spectacles of beauty, always changing their shape but retaining their clear blue ice, never ceased to amaze the Lindquists.

Fern Lindquist is an outstanding lecturer, and her lecture on Alaska, with accompanying slides, leaves one in breathless wonder. She shows the face of Mendenhall Glacier, on a 150-square-mile ice field near the capital city of Juneau, and describes how, in summer, ice slabs as high as six-story buildings wash down Mendenhall's face "with a roar to melt in a lake at its base." You can almost hear the roar and see this phenomenon.

She describes Mt. McKinley as drawing over 35,000 visitors annually to gaze at the peak that Indians centuries ago named "Denali," meaning "the great one." "Rightfully named," she states, "this tallest mountain in America —20,300 feet high—reigns majestically and could even be seen from our home in Anchorage.

"My throat literally ached with emotion as I gazed upon the silver-frosted peaks and ridges that stretched upward behind wispy clouds. Sometimes they were dressed in misty blue, sometimes robed in royal purple, other times decked out in strawberry pink! I felt like shouting David's words in Psalm 19:1: 'The heavens declare the glory of God; and the firmament showeth his handywork.'

"Tourists who think of Alaska only as a land of ice, snow, igloos, and Eskimos, are constantly amazed at the numerous varieties of wildflowers.

"Alaska also is a land where varied wild berries grow profusely, just begging to be picked.

"Where but in Alaska could we see a steaming volcano right from our living room windows? And where else but in Alaska could we ever view such a display of the aurora borealis spreading its pulsing veil over the skies? We'd run out into our yard just captivated and entranced by this solar-spawned phenomenon that streaked and shimmered in a variety of patterns in everchanging, multicolored bands.

"But all of this beauty was not what brought us to Alaska. It was in a small prayer group that Chapel by the Sea was born."

Chapel by the Sea: It was to become a major tourist attraction on the Seward Highway, drawing visitors from all over the world. How did it come about?

"The Lord performed five miracles for us to obtain the property with its three buildings in a needy and growing community. There was no for sale sign up, but one day as we were driving on the highway south of Anchorage, I encouraged my husband to inquire about the beautiful site we saw. I sat in the car and prayed!"

Miracle Number One: The maid who answered the door had just discovered that the people for whom she worked did not own the estate. They had given her that impression to discourage potential buyers like the Lindquists. "Perfect timing for us," Fern stated.

Miracle Number Two: "After learning that the former owners had both died five years previously, we wrote to the heir in Arizona. He had absolutely refused to sell up until that time. When we wrote, however, he was beginning to reconsider and wrote back suggesting that we make a proposal."

Miracle Number Three: "We offered him forty thousand dollars but with only a five thousand dollar down payment and at 6 percent instead of the going 8 percent rate of interest. He accepted the offer!"

Miracle Number Four: "My husband suggested to our smaller prayer group that we raised the initial five thousand dollars without borrowing. He passed out slips of paper and asked each one to prayerfully write down the amount they felt they could willingly give. When the slips were gathered, the round figure total was approximately five thousand dollars. None of these people were wealthy, and no one knew what the other person was putting down. Chapel by the Sea was born in the hearts of sacrificing people!"

Miracle Number Five: "One day the administrator of the estate phoned to inform us that in writing up the contract he wanted us, as buyers, to know that we must assume the costs of a lawsuit in case there was one. It seemed that some Alaska law protected the renter from having to move, and he could not be evicted. I responded to this by stating, 'We'll just pray them out.' And that's what we did. The day for moving arrived and the renters had shown no intention of moving. When we arrived with our truck and belongings, they quietly packed and left without a grumble and there was no lawsuit!

"That same evening our small group had a prayer and praise meeting. We had possessed the land. All glory to God."

Rex made it a policy never to go into debt for any improvements, and so it was with great rejoicing and gratitude that they saw things begin to take shape. They utilized the existing buildings to full advantage for Sunday School class-rooms and for chapel worship services.

The limited facilities began to fill and overflow. People drove from Anchorage, seven miles north, and from the Elmendorf Air Force Base and Fort Richardson Army Post, eleven miles north, and from as far as forty miles to the south to join in happy fellowship.

Soon they had to bulldoze a parking lot. Next they had to build a larger church structure. "Our men, with no intention of going into debt, by faith began digging a foundation. As the money came in, the boards went up, our own men doing the work, and the new structure became a reality."

Fern and Rex already knew from past experience that the Lord always blesses the local church which has a missionary vision. "At first we were somewhat afraid to bring in missionaries and ask our people (who were already giving far beyond a tithe) for an offering. So we would save some of our own offerings and tithes so we could give the missionary an offering and challenge the church with a missionary message. But then the people caught the missionary vision themselves and the giving just continued to increase."

Not only did the giving increase, but then the people themselves started going out as missionaries. "There was an indescribable spirit of love; many of these people were military people far away from home and loved ones. They found what they needed at Chapel by the Sea," the Lind-quists relate.

"We were one big happy family always doing things together. There was never a generation gap in the chapel." With much emotion Fern shows slides of the "little nuggets mined out of the hills and valleys surrounding the chapel in our first daily vacation bible school."

Most of the churches in Alaska are supported or partially aided by denominations in the "lower 48." "My husband determined from the start that this ministry would not be a recipient of mission funds but rather a propagator for missions. We were excited when our own people responded and felt compelled to go to faraway places with the Gospel and we could take over their support.

"God seemed to dare us to preach the pews empty—and we did lose couple after couple. Some went to other villages in Alaska such as Seldovia, Chignik, and Levelock, while others went to Panama, Viet Nam, the Bahamas, and Japan.

"The Lord quickly brought in others to fill their places in the Chapel by the Sea and to help in their prayer and financial backing.

"The Lord threw in an extra bonus when we acquired the property, for there was a thirty-by-fifteen-foot greenhouse that hadn't been in use for five years. That was a challenge to me. We cleaned it all up, and in February we turned on the heat and began planting all kinds of seeds in flats. Soon the seeds burst forth into a riot of colorful blooms in all their glory. They grew rapidly because there was no darkness in the summer months. They were growing while we were sleeping, so the first thing I did every morning was to run to the greenhouse to discover what had blossomed during the daylit night.

"We also grew luscious tomatoes—none in the stores could equal their delectable taste. At one point we had a one-and-a-half pound tomato! We even had corn on the cob.

"To my great amazement, the Lord took my gardening hobby and turned it into a ministry for his glory. Our gardens where chosen for eight consecutive years to be included in the annual Anchorage Garden Club Tour.

"Then the Tourist Information Bureau in Anchorage suggested to its inquirers that they stop at the Chapel by the Sea. And so they came, day after day after day. Automobiles, campers, trailers, motorcycles—every state in the Union was represented. One day as I looked out of my kitchen window, I noticed several tour buses stopping on the edge of our parking lot. I ran out to welcome them, inviting them to disembark. They were delighted! Every day after that they came, in sunshine or in the rain. As many as nine tour buses stopped daily—tour groups not only from the United States, but from Italy, Germany, Japan and, in fact, from every continent of the world. They parked right beside the chapel, they parked in front of our house, they parked wherever they could find room.

"I personally conducted tours—first taking them to see the beautiful mural of Mt. McKinley National Park in the chapel auditorium. People would kneel or sit reverently in the quietness as soft recorded organ music played in the background. The chapel was rustic, and people were intrigued by its simple beauty.

"Then to the greenhouse—naturally, this amateur gardener was delighted to hear their 'oohhs and aahhs'! They marveled at the giant glads and dahlias with geraniums in the front, all of the hundreds of plants ablaze in their brilliant color. Snapdragons, lobelia, sweetpeas, moss roses, and petunias added to the variety.

"Fragrant roses with no aphid worries flourished in the greenhouse as well as in planters alongside our house.

"I suppose we had the most photographed lemon tree in the world—for who would expect such a sight in Alaska? We plucked one lemon that made six lemon meringue pies, which I fed to the tour bus drivers.

"Rexine had tackled the immense grounds that had grown up in weeds due to the disinterest of the former occupants. With persistent hard work and God's sunshine and rain, the grounds took on a parklike appearance that brought enjoyment to the congregation as well as the visitors. The tourists explored our rock gardens with delight. They strolled on the kitchen walk to admire the dwarf twinkle phlox that bordered it and the glowing and blazing nemesia below the window. Hanging fuchsias thrived in the cool shade of the spruce trees.

"The visitors ambled along the garden paths. Begonias attracted the most interest as thirty thousand visitors trampled on the lawn to view them our last summer in Alaska. Over five hundred begonas were photographed as early as 2:30 A.M. and as late as 10 P.M.

"Even residents from Capitola, California, the begonia capital of the world, were amazed at the enormity of the blooms, some of which were larger than a person's face. All types of hanging begonias hung in rustic baskets alongside our log home.

"The enormous pansies captivated the sightseers attention bordering the side of the chapel in front of the aborvitae. But all of this gave opportunity for testimony and our chapel tract rack had to be constantly refilled."

During all this time in Alaska, Rex carried on a radio broadcast ministry over Anchorage's largest station, which reputedly reached three quarters of Alaska's population.

While in Alaska, Rex and Fern began the first of many trips, which took them to every continent except Australia, and to several islands of the sea. Fern's yen for travel became reality. The reason for the trips has been multifaceted—not only has it given them an opportunity to view first hand the missions work in which they have had such a vital interest and part through the years, but it has brought them together again with the individuals and families whom they have come to love so dearly in their "missions family" scattered around the world, and the slides they bring back are made into a travelogue presentation which Fern presents at every opportunity, thus challenging viewers to look upon these places as areas of the world in need of the message of Christ's love and salvation. When she makes such presentations, she comes dressed in the native costume of the land depicted.

Through the years Fern has acquired a collection of over one hundred bells from over fifty countries, but the emphasis is always on the Gospel message and a missionary challenge.

It was with many tears that the Lindquist family bade farewell on New Year's Eve, 1969, to the land and people they had come to love so very much. "My husband's aged parents needed to be cared for. We moved them to California, and Rex bought another Christian bookstore.

"Yes," she said thoughtfully, "Alaska became a beloved spot to us. There we witnessed eleven years of miracles—a church on a mission field becoming entirely self-supporting, giving over $125,000 to missions, never an appeal for money (for no offering plate was ever passed, just an offering box placed by the door). We saw it develop from an embryo to a mature body of believers.

"Lamentations 3:22 and 23 are our testimony: 'It is of the Lord's mercies that we are not consumed, because his compassions fail not. They are new every morning: great is thy faithfulness.' Yes, we, too, went to Alaska to discover gold and we did find it—in the lives of multitudes to whom we ministered, whose souls are worth more in the sight of our Lord than all the gold, silver, and oil in this fabulous north country."

When Rex was born his saintly grandmother gave him his name from Matthew 20:27—Rex, meaning king, and Steward, meaning servant. In Rex Lindquist we met a man who has dedicated himself unreservedly to serving others. We first met him at the Western Bible Book Store in Salinas, California, one of the most beautiful and finest stocked Christian bookstores it has been my privilege ever to see. Rex is a representative of that vast number—growing continually—of godly, dedicated people around the world who have felt called into a book ministry. These are men and women who are helping to change the world for Christ.

And Fern—what is she doing these days? "Rex has always appreciated an orderly house and a neat, orderly wife to greet him at the end of the day. I am to be the queen in our home, which I want to make a palace on earth for my king, Rex."

This she has done admirably. Walking into the Lindquist home is like going into an oasis, a beautiful museum where you feel right at home among the many lovely and unusual items which they have collected on their world travels. "Rex has always been a very busy man," she explains. "Because of this, our trips have been honeymoon vacations, where we discover not only the wonderful world God has made, but we rediscover ourselves. It is always such joy just to be with each other, holding hands as we ride on the plane, or run along the beach someplace." Theirs is a very special husband-wife relationship we observed. "We've had no quarrels in 39 years of marriage," she related. "When we disagree, we pray. Rex is usually always right," she added in a precious aside confession.

Leonard and Catherine Marshall LeSourd

7
Dreams Can Come True

AUTHOR
CATHERINE MARSHALL LeSOURD

Dreams can come true. Ask the successful and accomplished individual, regardless of the field of his or her endeavor, if they nurtured dreams through the years—dreams about what they wanted to do and be when they grew up—and almost without exception they will tell you that yes, such dreaming played an important part in shaping their destinies.

Just such a dreamer was the young girl, Catherine Wood. Readers the world over would recognize her today by the name of Catherine Marshall.

In writing circles there is an expression which carries much truth: I want to have written, but I don't want to write. Frequently, as writers, we hear individuals express the desire to someday write a book. More frequently than not such dreams never become reality. The reason? Writing is work. It's not only aspiration, it's inspiration and perspiration. It takes tremendous self-discipline and diligent application of one's mental and physical faculties to stick to the job at hand. Catherine Marshall LeSourd is that kind of woman—a dedicated, disciplined individual with a great God-given genius for transferring her thoughts, impressions, and feelings into words on paper. History will record her efforts as some of the finest literary achievements of our day. At the time of this writing there are more than 14 million hardcover and paperback copies of her thirteen books in print.

Yes, dreams can come true. In Catherine's case the dream took form early in her childhood. Once she began writing seriously in later life, following the death of her first husband, she discovered "the feel of paper and pencil in my hands—every bit of it was pure joy," as she says in her book *To Live Again* (p. 63).

In *To Live Again*, her fifth book, she describes the many things in the years gone by which she came to recognize had all been meant as preparation for writing and editing. Most writers are, first of all, readers. Catherine's father was a minister. Her love for reading was spawned in his book-lined study where the family gathered in the evening. "We did our reading and writing right there in father's study, and the warmth and happiness of the room became a part of the studying itself. Father and mother always near. . . . It was here that I started novels in notebooks that I bought for two for five cents. None progressed beyond the second or third chapters—but my dreams did.

"It was in that room that a love for books, for reading them, handling them, collecting them, even the dream of someday writing them, became part of my life" (pp. 63–64).

She remembers other moments from her childhood. She was standing at her bedroom window looking out, but not seeing, the mountain just across the valley. ' "For at that instant a dream was being planted in my heart. I had just finished a very girlish book, *Emily of New Moon*. The heroine wanted to be a writer; I had just discovered that I did, too."

In between the girlhood dream and its fulfillment, Catherine's life was, like some of the characters in the books she so enjoyed, to take on an almost storybook quality.

Her minister father's salary kept the family of five restricted to a very simple way of living. Still, Catherine's dream persisted.

In another of her books, *Adventures in Prayer*, she relates the heartache that engulfed her when she faced the fact that they were several hundred dollars short of the amount necessary to get her into Agnes Scott College in Decatur, Georgia. It was Depression time.

"One of the most provocative facts I know is that every manmade object, as well as most activity in your life and mine, starts with an idea or a picture in the mind. My mother first taught me this, and at the same time she vividly demonstrated to me the prayer that helps dreams come true. . . .

"One evening Mother found me lying across my bed, face-down, sobbing. She sat down beside me. 'You and I are going to pray about this,' she said quietly. We went into the guest room and knelt beside the old-fashioned, golden oak bed, the one that Mother and Father had bought for their first home. 'I know it's right for you to go to college,' Mother said. 'I believe God planted this dream in you; let's ask Him to tell us how to bring it to reality.'

"During those quiet moments in the bedroom, confidence and fresh determination flowed in. Mother's faith was contagious. The answer would come. How, we did not know.

"I went ahead and made preparations for Agnes Scott. A short time later, Mother received an offer from the Federal Writers' Project to write the history of the county. Her salary was enough to pay for the major part of my college expenses" (pp. 29–30).

Agnes Scott College, among other things, was to bring

Catherine into contact with a man called Peter. Sunday was the high point of the week for the lovely young Catherine. Even though it was a forty-minute streetcar ride from the college to Atlanta, Catherine wouldn't have missed going to Atlanta's Westminster Presbyterian Church for anything. The college crowd helped pack out the church Sunday after Sunday, and always Catherine watched the minister with adoring eyes. Georgia editorial comment was enthusiastic about the young Scottish minister. He was called that "charming young Scot with the silver tongue," and it was stated that "he was brilliant and witty," and many more superlatives, all underscoring the fact that he was an impressive, dramatic personality. But Catherine Wood could have added some strong impressions of her own.

He was not only all the things the newspapers said and the college crowd echoed, but he was plainly a much sought-after man.

Catherine, however, was a very attractive young woman. Then as now she had an inquiring mind with distinct tastes that were reflected in her manner of dress, her way of speaking, and in her every mannerism.

In her journals, which she had been keeping ever since she became an admirer of the writer Katherine Mansfield, she poured out her hopes and dreams. Her thoughts were later published in her book *A Man Called Peter*. "I have never met anyone whom I so want to know as Mr. Marshall," she wrote. In another entry she added, "Mr. Marshall conducts beautiful services, and I like him more each time I go.

"I have never heard such prayers in my life. It's as if, when he opens his mouth, there is a connected line between you and God. I know this sounds silly, but I've got to meet that man" (p. 61).

But Peter Marshall seemed almost "as inaccessible as a man from Mars," to Catherine. "Since I was very young and quite transparent," she relates, it "must have have been obvious to my parents that all of my idealism, as well as my naturally girlish romanticism, was rapidly centering upon this young Scottish minister."

She felt that Peter Marshall didn't even know she existed. When the time came for a personal encounter with the handsome and dignified Scotsman, at a Prohibition rally where they both spoke, Catherine was entirely unprepared for his comment when the chauffeur, Dr. Robinson, dropped her off. "May I see you sometime this week? I've wanted to know you for a long time."

Catherine's astonishment showed, and Peter Marshall quickly added, "Not even ministers are blind, you know."

Of their courtship Catherine wrote: "Six dates, four chaperones, and a dozen months later we were engaged.

"How it came about I still regard as one of God's nicest miracles and the first big evidence of God's hand on my life" (p. 63).

He was the embodiment of all her ideals, but he was twelve years older than she, and, in her words, "still as remote as the South Pole."

But not quite!

On a Sunday night in May, 1936, Peter Marshall knew that the beautiful young woman reviewing a book on prayer for Westminster's Fellowship Hour was the one for him. Catherine knew, too. She was so excited she had to get up and leave in what she called "the longest walk in history."

The college infirmary received her that night, and the next day Peter was over to see her. "He framed his proposal in gentle words," she wrote. But Catherine did not feel she could give him an immediate answer. "We agreed to pray about it separately. Years before, Peter's life had been solemnly dedicated to his Chief. Both of us felt that the important thing now was to find out what God wanted for us."

While her heart dictated the answer, she did not want it to obscure God's mind on the matter. "As unskilled and immature as I was in prayer, God chose this time to teach me a great lesson. I learned that just because God loves us so much, often He guides us by planting His own lovely dream in the barren soil of a human heart. When the dream has matured, and the time for its fulfillment is ripe, to our astonishment and delight, we find that God's will has become our will, and our will, God's. Only God could have thought of a plan like that" (pp. 68–69).

She graduated from Agnes Scott, and they were married in early November. Catherine wrote: "Dreams carried around in one's heart for years, if they are dreams that have God's approval, have a way suddenly of materializing" (p. 78).

Through the years of their marriage Peter Marshall came to value Catherine's suggestions, her research, her sensible criticism. And, during those years, Catherine never lost the dream she'd nurtured from childhood—she was a born writer.

Their son, Peter John, was born in 1940. Creativity had to be put aside as she took on the responsibilities of motherhood. But three years later Catherine was in bed with a widespread lung infection that was to last three years.

But these were years of enriching discoveries about herself—years of prayer and struggling to make her faith an effective instrument. When Catherine came to the moment when she placed her whole self in God's hands, there was a soul-deep spiritual change that was to alter her life completely. It meant giving up her own stubborn will; of giving her life over to the Living Christ to do with her as he would.

The years of confinement in bed were not wasted. Now she could read and write; now she helped Peter with his sermons more than ever. And once again, her own journals grew fat.

It was during this time that Catherine came across Hannah

Whitall Smith's book, *The Christian's Secret of a Happy Life*. Catherine would be the first to tell you that whereas Katherine Mansfield had introduced her to the idea of keeping a journal—and from her she absorbed much in the way of style and feminine insight—it was Hannah Whitall Smith who honed her spiritual insight.

From Peter, Catherine absorbed the belief that the Christian life is be joyous; now, reading *The Christian's Secret of a Happy Life*, Catherine's belief was reinforced. She decided then and there that she wanted to be like Hannah Whitall Smith. Anyone familiar with Hannah Smith's book and Catherine's book *Beyond Our Selves* will discover that she has succeeded.

The tremendous ministry that Peter Marshall enjoyed while at the historic New York Avenue Presbyterian Church in Washington, D.C., has been so beautifully chronicled by Catherine in that remarkable book *A Man Called Peter*. They had twelve glorious years as man and wife—years in which Dr. Marshall became chaplain of the United States Senate and one of the most revered men in America, years in which Catherine's happiness soared to undreamed of heights. She described those years in Peter's biography. "The years brought many changes for Peter and me. Into our marriage came an ever-deepening fusion of heart and mind, though never a static peace. It was a harmony growing out of diversity in unity, the most melodious harmony there is.

"His job was constantly to pour himself out for the hungry hearts of men and women. My job was to try to feed him spiritually, to strengthen him, to supply understanding and encouragement, so that he would always have something to give to others.

"We came to see this oneness between us as the open door by which the Spirit of God poured into our lives and work" (p. 238).

And then he was gone.

Now Catherine had to pick up the threads of her life and Peter John's, for life does go on. Then it was that God, in his infinite wisdom, began to show Catherine how he could use her long-nurtured dream. It was exactly what she needed to carry her through the next eleven years of widowhood. First there was the book of Peter Marshall's sermons, *Mr. Jones, Meet the Master,* and then *A Man Called Peter.*

She could not possibly know all that lay in store for her as a result of these first writing efforts. God's direction in her efforts was unmistakable. "No creative work," he told her, "has final impact unless it touches the reader at the level of the emotions." She adds, "As I worked on the manuscript of *A Man Called Peter,* he poured through me a stream of strong emotion."

God knows exactly whom he can entrust with these special gifts, and also the pain and sorrow. Catherine was a hand-maiden of the Lord in the most meaningful sense of the term, and she was equal to responding with intelligence, gracious-ness, courage and fortitude, and a loving warmth. She needed every God-given virtue, and she knew where her strength lay.

At the time of this writing there are more than 14 million hardcover and paperback copies of her thirteen books in print.

She explains: "I've simply been led from book to book. My experience has been unique in many ways. I've never had a single writing course in my life. I've never had a literary agent all these years, never had any need of one. I've been blessed with extremely fine editors who've taught me a great deal. So unique has the experience been that when would-be authors come to me for advice, it's a little embarrassing. I haven't gone the usual route. God's blessing is on this."

The phenomenal success of *A Man Called Peter* brought publicity and fame, leading to speeches—which she disliked with a passion—to autograph parties, Hollywood, and Success (rightly spelled with a capital S).

"The Spirit became my instructor in creative writing. He took me by the hand and showed me that the opening pages must present Peter Marshall in the framework in which the public knew him—through his Senate chaplaincy. Only then could I flash back to Peter's early life and come forward."

Six books later Catherine wrote another best seller, *To Live Again*, which told how, in her words, her "world caved in." It was a monumental work describing in a painfully honest way that out of loneliness can come love, that "out of the heart's need" one can creep humbly back "to acknowledge that need and to rejoin the human race."

Book number seven took its place on the nation's bestseller lists, and once again readers around the world were to be blessed and helped. "At moments when the future is completely obscured, I thought, can any one of us afford to go to meet our tomorrows with dragging feet? God had been in the past. Then He would be in the future, too.

"And with His presence had always come an end to tasteless living. Always He had brought adventure—high hopes, unexpected friends, new ventures that broke old patterns. Then out in my future must lie more goodness, more mercy, more adventures, more friends" (*Adventures in Prayer*, pp. 33–38).

Son Peter John was growing up. Catherine let her readers in on what had been happening with him, too, through the years.

But now what?

In her heart of hearts Catherine wanted to write a novel. The idea for *Christy* had been brewing in her thinking for some time. She and her mother had even made two trips back into the region where that book had its setting. But this was not God's timing.

It was in the autumn of 1953 that Catherine was first to

meet Leonard Earle LeSourd. She was the visiting speaker at Norman Vincent Peale's Marble Collegiate Church in New York. The man who was to successfully woo and win the much-sought-after Catherine Marshall was in the crowd that evening.

Six years later they were married in Leesburg, Virginia, in a ceremony officiated at by three clergymen: her father, Leonard's father, and Norman Vincent Peale.

Leonard LeSourd was an editor and a self-effacing gentleman. He moved in on the unsuspecting Catherine in just the right way. God's hand was in it all. Catherine had been courted in the most gallant way by a number of interested suitors through the years, but always she had maintained a certain aloofness. In his own quiet unassuming way, the much-respected editor of *Guideposts* magazine changed all that.

In book number eight, written two years after their marriage, Catherine said: "The Kingdom of God is the kingdom of right relationships." Leonard LeSourd was the right relationship.

Through reading Hannah Smith's book *The Christian's Secret of a Happy Life,* Catherine had made the grand life-changing discovery that "the Christian life must be lived in the will, not in the emotions." But now, once again, Catherine's emotions were allowed to become involved as she felt her heart responding to the love of Leonard LeSourd.

And then there were Leonard's three children—Linda, who was nine; Chester, five; and Jeffrey, two. "Len was quite ready to marry again," she states, and she knew that so was she.

There were adjustments. But they were met in the serene atmosphere of mutual love, respect and deep understanding. They discovered that their careers meshed very well. Len was magnificently empathetic, generous with praise, and valuable in counsel.

Catherine accepted the challenge of raising three more children as "unto the Lord," and relinquished her will to "accept what had to be accepted" in "creating an atmosphere of security for these children who badly needed it." In acceptance lieth peace. Catherine knew it. Leonard knew it. Together they accepted the responsibilities; the adjustments that must be made were confronted and met as they walked hand in hand into the future, open to receive all that God had in his creative plan for their lives now as a family.

Book number eight, *Beyond Our Selves,* took its rightful place alongside the other Catherine Marshall books in stores across the nation.

Then came the move to Florida, necessitated by Catherine's lung condition. Still Catherine could not rid herself of the desire to complete the manuscript on *Christy.* It was a battlefield, a fight all the way.

It took nine years of painstaking work, research, rewrite, and a juggling of all the elements that comprise this brilliantly written novel (which she says is 65 percent true—much of it based on her mother's life). It was an achievement, another miracle of God-blessed creativity.

Thirteen years were to pass between the writing of *Beyond Our Selves* and Catherine's next major achievement. *Something More* reached the hands of the ever eager Catherine Marshall devotees in 1974. The publishers described this volume as an "inimitable blend of autobiography, dramatic narrative, and Biblical lesson that has earned her literally millions of readers since the publication of *A Man Called Peter* in 1951." And that it is!

We discovered that the children were now grown and gone from the security of the family nest. To our surprise we realized that Peter John was no longer the train-loving little boy of the Washington manse—why we still imagined him that way I do not know! Now Peter John was himself a father and a minister. Catherine and Leonard were also proud grandparents. Yes, the years had successfully wrought change. We found out, too, that Catherine's mother was still living at Evergreen Farm in Loudoun County, Virginia. And we learned, sadly, that once again Catherine had faced death—this time the death of two grandchildren.

Not surprisingly, Catherine was her usual honest self. But there were fresh insights and humor. "You and I are living in rough times," she wrote. "We must make our way through minefields of evil, booby traps of deception, brush fires of sickness and disease, wastelands of economic disaster, burning deserts of disappointment. 'I won't take you out of this world,' Jesus told us. 'But don't be afraid, because I've overcome that world of dangers. All power is Mine. I promise to be with you always.' "

Then she asked the question hovering always on the lips of so many. " 'How, Lord? How are you with us?'

" 'Through the Helper.'

"It is true. He is here. We who in moments of desperation have asked, 'What can I do? What is there left?' have felt His answering presence and experienced His help. . . . We know now . . . always He holds out to us the exciting promise of something more."

The ink was hardly dry on *Something More* when, in 1975, a slim, beautifully illustrated volume in sepia tones was on the bookstore shelves. I picked it up and knew that in my hands I held a rich treasure. *Adventures in Prayer* lived up to the promise of its name. "It will become a classic," I told my husband. She talks of the prayer of helplessness, the prayer that helps your dreams come true, the waiting prayer, the prayer of relinquishment, the prayer in secret, the prayer of joyous blessing, and the claiming prayer.

I knew she was in the process of writing these two books, for we had been in correspondence. What were the LeSourds up to now, I wondered. "We have just moved the base of our operations from Florida to Virginia," Leonard said in his May 1975 letter.

Now he was no longer editor of *Guideposts*, but together they and John and Elizabeth Sherrill, well-known writers, had restructured a venture called Chosen Books into a new partnership with headquarter offices in Lincoln, Virginia.

In 1955 Catherine bought Evergreen Farm, a 143-acre place for her parents' retirement. With the death of her father in 1961 and advancing years for her mother, it was either sell the farm or move there themselves. They chose the latter.

"Leonard," I wrote, "please describe the Catherine of today for her readers who love her so." This he did as only a loving husband could do so tenderly. "She is about 5 foot 3, with soft reddish-brown hair. She has tremendous inner intensity and drive, although her lung trouble has made her reduce her physical activities. She has very blue eyes out of which sparks often fly on all manner of subjects and issues. Her very feminine qualities are mixed with this intensity—an intriguing combination. She is pragmatic and yet this, too, is blended with an intense seeking of the Holy Spirit at all times."

William Gildea, writing in *The Washington Post*, June 1, 1976, describes the Catherine of today as appearing to be "a strong, determined person; she is formal, almost proper, not frivolous in the least. She gives the impression an interview may be more effort than pleasure."

Does Catherine Marshall LeSourd have time for anything besides writing and overseeing their Virginia and Florida homes? "She is really talented with her paints," her husband says, "and has come up with half a dozen oils that have been framed and hang on relatives' and friends' walls." They are mostly pastoral scenes.

Other hobbies include gardening. "Especially roses," she says, "and a great variety of fruit trees in Florida."

She enjoys needlepoint, "and the fun of a variety of handicrafts, such as painting toy chests, bedroom furniture, and making doll clothes for my grandchildren."

And she is a collector, "especially of cherished recipes," she relates.

Catherine and Leonard begin the day at 6:30 by reading the Bible together and praying. They use notebooks to list who and what they are praying for.

Leonard says she does her "hard manuscript work in the mornings. Afternoons are usually devoted to research, answering mail, and she'll also take an hour's nap."

And what of Leonard LeSourd himself? "Len is of medium height with an athletic build resulting from what hours he is able to spend on the tennis courts. With his lean face and grey hair, he might be described as distinguished-looking in his more serious moments. Although his speech is quiet, there is an inner glow and humor that quite frequently comes through, especially in hectic situations."

The LeSourd's secretary, Jeanne Sevigny, added some insights on both of them: "Leonard and Catherine are in complete accord that Jesus Christ is Lord of every aspect of their lives, and they serve him faithfully, the intensity of Catherine balanced by the quiet inner strength of Len. Each day they seek the guidance of the Holy Spirit for their own situation and in ministering to those around them."

Yes, dreams can come true. Catherine Marshall LeSourd is surely a case in point. "All such dreaming is, in a sense, praying," she maintains. "It is certainly the Creator's will that the desires and talents that He Himself has planted in us be realized. God is supremely concerned about the fulfillment of the great person He envisions each of us. He wants us to catch from Him some of His vision for us. After all, this is what prayer is, men cooperating with God in bringing from heaven to earth His wondrously good plans for us.

"In fact, there is no limit to what a combination of dreams and prayer can achieve.

"Hand your dream over to God, and then leave it in His keeping. There seem to be periods when the dream is like a seed that must be planted in the dark earth and left there to germinate. This is not a time of passiveness on our part. There are things we can and must do—fertilizing, watering, weeding—hard work and self-discipline.

"But the growth of that seed, the mysterious and irresistible burgeoning of life in dark and in secret, *that* is God's part of the process. We must not keep digging up our dream, examining it and measuring it to see how it is coming along.

"But in the meantime, long before we see the fruition of our hopes, in fact the very moment a God-given dream is planted in our hearts, a strange happiness flows into us. I have come to think that at that moment all the resources of the universe are released to help us. Our praying is then at one with the will of God, a channel for the Creator's always joyous, triumphant purposes for us and our world."

"It's amazing," she says, "to earn a living doing the thing you enjoy doing, with the added dividend of being helpful to many people." Just how helpful she has been she will never know on this side of heaven, but multitudes of people would agree that they are glad and thankful that Catherine Marshall LeSourd dared to dream, and that God has been in it all.

Lionel and Dorothy Mayell

8
Little Is Much with God

CAMPUS CRUSADE'S
LIONEL MAYELL

It was 1948. The directors for Christ for Greater Los Angeles were meeting to decide who would be their speaker for their upcoming crusade. One of the directors presented the name of a young evangelist by the name of Billy Graham. Opposition was outspoken. "Why, he's not even known," someone said. Another remarked, "Los Angeles is a large sophisticated city, let's not forget it. That young man wouldn't have sufficient know-how and what it takes to draw crowds."

The director who had thrown Billy Graham's hat in the ring spoke up one more time. "Gentlemen," he said, drawing himself up full stature, "the precious Holy Spirit can bring the crowds, and with the right kind of publicity by us with each one of us inspired by the Holy Spirit, we can have capacity attendance and see Christ uplifted."

Today that gentleman says, "I lost. The directors voted to wait until Billy Graham became better known."

One week later, however, the directors of Youth for Christ were meeting in Los Angeles. "I was a member of that board also," the man explains. "Every year for many years Youth for Christ endeavored to have one big rally in the great Shrine Auditorium. In 1948 we discussed moving this to Hollywood Bowl, which would hold more than double the capacity of the shrine. Again I presented the name of Billy Graham to this board, and the Holy Spirit took my words, and the board approved and invited young Billy Graham to be the speaker at this one-night stand in Hollywood Bowl."

The night for this great special meeting arrived in the fall of 1948. Before the time for the opening of the meeting the bowl was jammed to the perimeter. "There must have been twenty to twenty-five thousand persons there. At the close of his great message hundreds poured down the aisles and climbed over seats to reach the altar. Los Angeles had never seen such numbers at an altar call up until this time.

"Immediately following this great Youth for Christ meeting, the Christ for Greater Los Angeles Board convened again. This time the decision was unanimous to invite Billy Graham to return the next year for a great city-wide revival." That meeting was to go down in history as Graham's first major crusade in the United States.

Who was that man who had such confidence in the then comparatively unknown twenty-four-year-old evangelist Billy Graham? Small in stature, but a Holy-Spirit-filled dynamo known and beloved around the world as Lionel Mayell.

I have never seen Lionel in anything but perpetual motion. Since 1965 he has been a familiar figure around the Campus Crusade for Christ headquarters in the San Bernardino mountains. "Seeing a man of Lionel's age working in a predominantly youth-oriented organization is about as surprising as seeing your grandfather head back to school to earn a college degree," wrote Al Janssen of Lionel Mayell in the CCC publication *Worldwide Challenge*. "He possesses so much energy that Campus Crusade staff in their twenties have trouble keeping up with him."

At the time of that writing Lionel was seventy-eight years young.

Often when I have been with Lionel and his remarkable wife, Dorothy, I have been reminded of another well-known man of whom the Bible states, "he was little of stature." Zacchaeus was his name. He was the "chief among the publicans," the receiver-general of the customs, that is, with many other publican officers under him. Not surprisingly for one in this position, Zacchaeus was a very rich man. Those who knew him best called Zacchaeus "a notorious sinner." And that's where the similarity between Lionel Mayell and the tax collector does not jibe.

Whereas Lionel has made and lost two fortunes in his illustrious lifetime, he attained to this by dint of hard work, using his head and directing his energies in constructive ways that would, as a result, amass for him a financial empire and the right to be called a millionaire by the time he was thirty-two.

Matthew Henry, the Bible commentator, says that "many who are little of stature have large souls, and are lively in spirit." That description fits Lionel Mayell. Lionel, and Zacchaeus, too, took every advantage to raise themselves to a sight of Christ. And in the doing, they were not ashamed to admit their need. They aimed high to reach high, and God rewarded them. Those who have a mind to know Christ shall be known of him. Those who are faithful in their little shall be entrusted with more. The story of Zacchaeus is recorded in Luke 19. The story of Lionel Mayell cannot be recorded in a mere chapter but can best be seen in the lives of people who have been touched by his eagerness to introduce them to Jesus, and who have seen the love of Jesus in Lionel.

It was a frigid cold wintry morning in London, Ontario,

Canada, when Lionel was born. His mother took one look at the four pounds plus a few ounces, wrinkled, red, tiny thing the nurse was holding and commented, "It's more like monkey than man!"

But the screaming little baby survived. The elder Mr. Mayell was associated with his father in a manufacturing and wholesale grocery business. In 1909 they moved to Los Angeles. "We lived under the very eaves of the University of Southern California," he recalls. "Our neighbors lived in large two- and three-story grand houses, ornate and beautifully designed for the day, located on a wide avenue, bordered by stately old pepper trees with their gnarled trunks. Several of our neighbors were to become famous in Los Angeles over the decades to come—the Robinsons three doors to the north founded the Robinson Department Stores of southern California; and next to them was old Mr. Ralph, beloved by all who knew him, who was to found the Ralph Grocery Store Chain; and just across the street was neighborly Mr. Hagarty of the exclusive Hagarty Department Stores.

"We all had our own one-horse surreys. My grandfather himself lived among his great orange trees, large beds of fabulous rose bushes, and hundreds of busy bees which he dearly harbored and loved. He was the subject of Jean Stratton Porter's novel, *The Keeper of the Bees*."

Lionel's grandfather delighted in listening to his grandson's chatter. "You know, Leon," he would say to this animated child, "although you think of me as a very old man, I actually feel as young as you. I just can't run like a fox like you do, is all, and I can't do many things that I once did and would like to do now!" The old gentleman lived to be ninety-six.

Lionel's mother was an avid Bible student with deep study in both Hebrew and Greek. "She attended Biola College within two years after it was founded. For some time she traveled in the evangelistic team of Dr. W. E. Biederwolf in charge of the women's work, expounding the Word in Sunday afternoon Bible studies while Biederwolf preached to the male benefactors.

"My father, too, was a very dynamic Christian businessman. We lived for a time about two blocks from the residence of Dr. R. A. Torrey," Lionel recalls.

"Many precious hours were spent back and forth between the two homes. My mother was not only an outstanding and challenging Bible student and speaker, but she wrote in many Christian publications. One of her friends was Dr. Henrietta Mears, and it was in the late Miss Mears's home that we first met Bill and Vonette Bright. At that time Bill was manufacturing candy and leasing and selling cars so he could attend seminary.

"Dr. Charles Fuller, who organized what was to become the world-known radio broadcast 'The Old Fashioned Revival Hour,' was one of my father's best friends."

Lionel rattles names off that read like a "Who's Who in the Christian World" from a bygone era. "Dr. C. I. Scofield, Peter Billhorn, Dr. William Evans (father of Dr. Louis Evans, Sr.), Mel Trotter, Dr. Cortland Meyers, Dr. James McGinley, Dr. Bullinger, Dr. Sperry Chaffer, and numerous great preachers of the last seventy-five years frequently came to our home for small and large dinners, for Bible studies, or as friends to fraternize over the Bible, the signs of the times, and the authority of the Word."

In 1916 Lionel enrolled in Occidental College. "Our prexy was Dr. Willis Bear, a giant in great spiritual faith. During my stay at Occidental I met many who became lifelong friends—Captain Paul Leavens and his lovely wife, Anne, great pillars of the Christian faith in southern California; Cameron Townsend; and Buddy Robinson." Cameron

Townsend was the founder of Wycliffe Bible Translators, and Buddy Robinson was the missionary who, along with Cameron, went as a free-lance missionary to Guatemala years ago.

"One of my good friends during Occidental days was Louis Evans. At that time (1917) he was one of the outstanding football lettermen. He was one of our early strong Christian athletes, became an All-American letterman, and won great ovations for his college and for the Lord.

"Dr. Sam Sutherland, another great friend at Occidental, soon won his doctorate, and with Dr. Louis Talbot reorganized Biola as it moved from central Los Angeles to La Mirada. It was Dr. Talbot who married my wife, Dorothy, and myself in 1943.

"Dr. Louis Evans was to go on and become the minister of the largest Presbyterian church in the world, First Presbyterian of Hollywood."

Lionel's mother insisted upon his studying Greek with Dr. J. H. Allen. "Mother planned it this way to see to it that I became a Christian, but this plan of hers didn't work out for I didn't become a born-again Christian until many years later."

Following Occidental, young Lionel took up the study of law at the University of California and then went on to study it at Stanford. While at Stanford he became enthralled with the great co-op apartments being built in New York City and many large cities in the east. As a result of this and subsequent investigation and of making the right contacts, Lionel explains, "With God's help I began a $100 million program covering over fifty years." Actually this was to lead to Lionel's becoming the father of the own-your-own-apartment concept, today known around the world as the condominium.

Even though he had not given his life to Christ, Lionel was

a God-fearing man. "The John Wanamaker story inspired me. John was an office boy in the office of an insurance agent who was a Christian. On the desk of this Christian businessman was a bronze plaque which said: 'Without faith it is impossible to please God: for he that cometh to God must believe that he is, and that he is a rewarder of them that diligently seek him' " (Heb. 11:6).

That Wanamaker biography intrigued Lionel, and that verse stayed with him. "The 'reward' portion of this verse greatly impressed me. I thought the Lord would 'reward' me with money if I diligently sought him." Of course, Lionel's motives at that point were wrong, but God does see into our hearts. Deep inside this man's heart God read other intent, and God, who knows the end from the beginning, was going to reward Lionel in his own way.

"I really was convinced that I couldn't amount to much," he confesses. "I didn't feel I possessed a large amount of intellect; I'm not brainy; I'm not brilliant." (There are those, however, who would like to dispute that with the modest Mayell.)

"So every time someone came to buy one of my apartments, I bathed it in prayer to God. I'd say, 'You are going to reward me because I am diligently seeking you and in myself I can do nothing.' "

Then Lionel would think of the famous Philadelphia financier John Wanamaker and the biography that so inspired him, and, highly motivated, he would press on in his ventures. By 1929, at the age of twenty-three, he had completed his first large nine-story building with nearly 2 million dollars in apartment house sales value. At the age of thirty-two his apartment buildings aggregated $10 million.

"The Great Depression came in like a black cloud forboding of death. I knew that I could no longer finance, build, or sell my beautiful luxurious apartment homes for some time. I then traveled throughout Spain introducing my apartment concept which was the beginning of the Spanish condominium."

His nature was ever restless. "I could not remain inactive," he relates, "and not yet knowing the Lord Jesus Christ in a personal way, I interested myself in becoming active in show business. I would put an electrical extravaganza on the road." And that, indeed, is what it was! "There were fourteen huge stages being transported from arena to arena on a chartered train of locomotives with fourteen flat cars, and we used a tugboat with fourteen flat boats going down the Mississippi. Hundreds of beautiful girls engaged in various contests in many cities and manned the floats in a gorgeous exhibition. The presentation cost $25 thousand nightly, and 500 storage batteries beneath each float were to brilliantly illuminate them. A total of seven thousand batteries were exhausted of their energy nightly and had to be recharged the next day! Top stars of the performances included Jean Harlow, Bebe Daniels, Robert Taylor, Rudy Vallee, and Ginger Rogers.

"Great profits were made when the weather remained fair, but in a few months we had sufficient rainy and bad weather to put my lovely show out of business and upwards to a million dollars were sunk in Satan's inspired show."

Not even the fact that the governor of Texas hailed Mayell as "the world's greatest showman" and presented him with an engraved plaque could compensate for the fact that this venture ended in failure. Lionel left the Cotton Bowl of Dallas. "I didn't have enough money to purchase a cup of coffee after buying a bus ticket back to California."

Never down for long, Lionel soon bounced back with another business idea, again in the apartment building area. "I called on the manager of one of the Banks of America and asked to borrow on an unsecured note. I stated that I had built many large apartment buildings and believed the war was about over, for many of our reconnaissance flyiers were returning from the Far East and reporting that a new piece of war hardware had been invented and would soon be un- leashed upon Japan, bringing her to her knees.

" 'It's time for me to be planning my future in the apart- ment business once again,' I told the bank manager.

" 'Mr. Mayell, I know much about your fine business op- erations in Long Beach and Los Angeles and we will be very happy to loan you money on an unsecured note.'

"I went home on cloud nine," he says. " 'I'm going down tomorrow and deposit $1,000 in a new business account,' I told Dorothy. But a few weeks before this, Dorothy had sug- gested that we take our two children down to a Youth for Christ meeting. This was a new program held at the Church of the Open Door in Los Angeles, and it was geared to youth.

"We both thought this would be a good idea to get our kids off the streets at least one evening a week. But little did we realize that both of us were to receive Christ at one of the Youth for Christ rallies.

"When I told Dorothy that I was depositing $1,000 to be- gin our new business, she said, 'Daddy, we are Christians now and Christ is our partner. I think we should take $500 of this money and place it in an account for the work of our Savior, Jesus Christ; and the remaining $500 can go in your new business account. This will be one way of showing our love for Christ.'

"I responded to that by stating, 'But just what can I do to start a business with only $500?'

"Dorothy was quick to suggest, 'I would greatly prefer to be a partner with God with half of all we have invested in his work, and the remainder in a business account, than to leave him out in the cold with nothing from us for his great work.'

"She won out, and we opened up two accounts with the $1,000 from the bank loan."

How God works is a constant marvel to the Mayells! One

evening at a Youth for Christ meeting shortly thereafter Lionel took out the checkbook for the Lord's account and wrote out a check to the organization for $500. In the upper left-hand corner of the check he wrote: "To help start Youth for Christ work in the Orient."

Dorothy was puzzled when Lionel handed her the check to sign. "Why are you doing this?" she asked. "Nobody has talked about such an undertaking," she commented.

"Sweetheart, just sign the check," was all Lionel said.

The following weekend Bob Pierce, who was founder of World Vision International, and Dave Morken attended a great YFC Rally in St. Petersburg, Florida. It rained cats and dogs. But nevertheless it was a great rally; the thousands in attendance were saturated with rain, but they were also saturated with something else. No, someone else, would be more accurate.

The love of God in Christ Jesus rained down upon all in attendance as Bob Pierce and Dave Morken told how their prayers of ten years had been answered the previous Saturday night in Los Angeles at a YFC Rally when a little, inconspicuous couple had given $500 to "help start YFC work in the Orient." For many years, many heads of various mission boards and Chinese churches had asked Bob and Dave to plan meetings and raise support so that they could go into China before Communism put down the bamboo curtain.

At the close of this rainy session, an old man, dripping wet, came up to Dave Morken and handed him a wet envelope. "At two the next morning, Dave remembered and jumped out of bed and retrieved the envelope from his wet topcoat. He tore it open and found a check payable to them for the sum of $5,000 and in a pencil notation in the left corner of the check: "To help start work in the Orient.' Lionel's little $500 check and this man's $5,000 check sent Bob Pierce and Dave Morken to China. Hundreds received Christ, and great evangelistic rallies were held all over the Orient before it fell under Communism.

"This was the beginning of World Vision in which more than twenty thousand orphans found Christ and Korea, likewise, heard the Gospel. This was the first fruit of our little $500 gift.

"The remaining little $500 deposit in our business account, with Christ as our partner, was the beginning of the $100 million Lionel Mayell Enterprise of condominium apartment homes. Yes, our great God has more than carried out his promise 'that he is a rewarder of them who diligently seek him,' and 'he will do exceedingly more than you can even ask or think.' "

The new construction empire was flourishing. World War II was over and with the return of veterans, true to Lionel's prediction, the need for homes for these men and their families became a tremendous factor in boosting sales. Mismanagement by business partners, however, saw the fall of the empire. Lionel himself however emphatically states that it was God who took his money away. "It all happened very smoothly. I had no lawsuits. I never had to go into bankruptcy. God just took it away."

Of course he was crushed by the series of events at first. He even prayed to the Lord, upholding what he felt were his virtues, and asking why.

Lionel Mayell is one of the most astonishingly candid people you'll ever meet. He's been described as talking at the speed of an auctioneer, and you'll always know right where he stands on any issue. So when Lionel had thoroughly exercised himself in prayer to the Lord seeking an answer to why suddenly he found himself at the bottom once again without financial security and his business gone, you know he's being honest when he tells you, "God showed me I was bragging."

His explanation? "God has plainly said in his Word, 'I will

not share my glory with anybody,' and he made it very clear that I'd been living it up all those years, priding myself on my wealth and thinking what a great guy I was in giving the Lord all the credit. I was doing nothing of the sort—I was taking the glory back to myself, Lionel Mayell. I was an egotist. God is no respector of persons."

The magnificent family home in Los Angeles is gone. But the pleasant memories remain—the hospitality which the Mayells extended to members of the Billy Graham Team and their wives during the historic 1949 Christ for Greater Los Angeles meetings has resulted in friendships that have endured and grown sweeter through the years. Perhaps one of the most memorable events through the years (and there have been many) was this first Billy Graham Crusade. Lionel likes to tell about it, because it so powerfully demonstrates God's goodness and greatness, and the remarkable answer to prayer that occurred.

"A huge tent—a Ringling Brothers Circus tent—was erected on the corner of Washington and Hill Streets in Los Angeles. The tent contained 6,600 seats. It was September of 1949."

Actually September in southern California is generally regarded as one of the hottest times of the year. Not so in 1949. "It was the coldest weather of any September in weather bureau history up to that time. The penetrating winds didn't help the situation any either. The flaps of the huge tent had to be spiked to the floor; several large gas furnaces were installed in the rafters of the tent. Although well advertised, there were seldom more than 2,500 persons attending the meetings because of the severe cold.

"A meeting was called for 4 P.M. on the last Sunday of the final week of the three-week crusade. Billy said he had preached all of the sermons that he had prepared, but that the Lord would give him more if the meetings continued.

Some pointed out that if the bad weather persisted, the Christ for Greater Los Angeles organization would go bankrupt. But it was pointed out that the Lord had been present and several thousand decisions had resulted from these first three weeks and that there were many people who had been coming and were coming back and who were under great conviction, and who, if the meetings continued, would receive Christ.

"At 7:20 P.M. that Sunday evening hundreds began to pour into the tent, but still no decision had been made by the board authorizing Billy to stop or to announce that the meetings would continue on. It was almost 7:30 P.M., and still no decision. The air was tense. I arose from the back row and made a motion that carried unanimously.

"To the best of my knowledge, as I recall, this is what I said: 'Gentlemen, without question bad weather has seemingly destroyed our faith. We know that Satan does not want these great meetings to continue. God has given us great preaching through Billy Graham. The Lord has proven to us his great pleasure with the fruit of Billy's ministry, for even with the small crowds we've had, the greatest altar calls have been made and we've never before seen such response. The Lord controls all things.

" 'Well do we remember that Christ broke up the storm on the lake when the boat was about to sink. He is our great Lord and Savior and does not wish that any should perish, but that all should be brought to salvation. Therefore, I move that if our great and mighty Lord should see fit to change the weather this night, within one hour from now, when Billy will just about be closing his sermon, if there is a noticeable change in the weather, Billy will be authorized to announce that the meetings will continue from week to week as the Lord leads.' "

Lionel continues the amazing, little-known story: "Before

8:20 P.M. that last Sunday evening of the three weeks Christ for Greater Los Angeles Crusade in 1949, all of the women began fanning themselves. Billy had to stop preaching and ask the janitor to open up the flaps in the tent and let some fresh air in. He then asked the engineer to bring in the ladder and turn off the furnaces. He completed his sermon. He had a great altar call and then announced that the meetings would continue from week to week.

"From that night on the weather changed and several thousands more came down to the altar nightly to receive Christ. Among the number was Stuart Hamblin (the cowboy musician and songwriter best known for *It Is No Secret*) and former wiretapper Jim Vaus. It was heralded as one of the greatest Crusades that Christ for Greater Los Angeles had ever had."

These are tender memories that time has not dimmed. Lionel could tell you many more.

In 1965 when Campus Crusade for Christ International created a military ministry to assist chaplains in ministering to military personnel and their families, Lionel and Dorothy Mayell were invited to come on staff. Each of the more than 4,500 staff members of CCC must raise his own financial support. This was a switch for the Mayells. "It took two-and-a-half years to do this," they relate, "primarily because most of our friends couldn't believe that we no longer had any money. They thought for sure we had something stashed away." But in 1966, with their support raised, they made the move.

Since then Lionel and Dorothy have been able to do everything together as a team. Dorothy helped raise Lionel's children by his first marriage, and then the Lord blessed them with three of their own. Both Lionel and Dorothy are greatly loved and appreciated for their personal humility and willingness to care for others. Each throws all of their energies into helping those who are assigned to them for discipline and nurture—a convicted teenage murderer of seven people, a former top man in Hell's Angels, businessmen, and high-ranking military officials.

In recent years the Mayells have worked closely with Colonel Heath Bottomly and his wife, Betty, and other members of the family, in counseling and helping them become rooted and established into things of the Lord. Bottomly was known in the service as the Warlord of Southeast Asia, commandeering the largest airbase in the war.

The situation with Colonel Bottomly tried Lionel Mayell's patience to the utmost, but true to his nature, Lionel stuck with this assignment. Patiently and persistently, Lionel led the colonel into an understanding of the Word. One night, in the presence of another military man, Colonel Bottomly picked up Lionel and threw him into a swimming pool. Lionel sputtered his way to the top and, not knowing exactly what Bottomly would do next, treaded water. Then, leaning on the side of the pool, he said very firmly: "Colonel, I am greatly disappointed at your lack of what it takes, for I thought you could at least throw me into the center of the pool rather than a mere four feet from the perimeter. Try again and see if you can do a little better."

That seemed to break the ice, and from that time on their relationship deepened. The Colonel related how he had met Christ during a personal crisis in Vietnam. "I told him that I could see he was an experienced speaker and that he should prepare his testimony and honor the Lord by giving it whenever the opportunity presented itself. It wasn't long before he agreed to become a member of the Associate Staff of Campus Crusade for Christ International and took the required training." From that time up to the present, the Colonel has spoken before more than 200,000 people; a film has been made of his life; and a biography has been written. Lionel continues to be the Colonel's spiritual adviser; he is just one of many whom it has been Lionel's privilege and responsibility to help in his capacity at Campus Crusade for Christ.

Dorothy Mayell has been the devoted wife, "tremendous companion, sweetheart, mother and the sweet inspiration of the home" to Lionel and the children. "She lives to bring happiness and spiritual values at all times to everyone with whom she comes in contact," Lionel said in paying tribute to this gracious woman who has been at his side since 1943. I personally know that she is greatly beloved by everyone who has had occasion to work with her—in Bible classes, in counseling, and in everything else.

Dr. Bill Bright and his wife, Vonette, in writing of the Mayells said: "They are such special people. This family is one of the most genuine Christian families we know. They live what they proclaim. We have found them solid in every kind of circumstance, continually bringing honor and glory to the Lord. Their lives minister to us constantly.

"They have made such a fantastic transition into a modest life-style after generously supporting full-time Christian workers for so many years and now finding themselves in a situation where they have to raise support. Many people have found it difficult to believe they have not had resources beyond their Campus Crusade salary. They give so much of themselves to people and so generously share everything they have, even at times when it is very little. I know of no couple who have such significant ministries in the lives of others."

In March, 1975, Lionel was placed under rigid doctor's control. In correspondence since then he states: "The Lord has given us so many thrilling experiences, and the older we get, the more I find myself frequently going back over many of these occasions.

"Now I am trying to live under doctor's rules but find it

nearly impossible. I do enjoy working so much, so I am depending upon the Lord for my strength.

"My cardiologist warns me not to spend more than four hours each day at work or risk a stroke or heart attack, but I have told him that my Lord and Savior holds the span of my life in his hands and that I would not be living at all if I were to be relegated to only four hours each day for his honor and his glory. Well do I know that my salvation in no way depends upon the work I fail to do or succeed in doing. And he does not necessarily want my work but wants me to continually grow more and more like him."

Gratitude is a shining quality radiating from Lionel and Dorothy Mayell. Lionel himself would say, "I know I'm expendable. God can use any one of us if we'll just let him, even a little aging runt like me."

I rather think that if Jesus came to San Bernardino, California, and the crowd was as great as it was that day in Jericho so long ago, that one little man, like Zaccheus, would be very undignified and scramble up a tree in his eagerness to see this one. It wouldn't matter what people said or thought. And Jesus would look up and say, "Come down, Lionel, I want to be a guest in your home today."

Stanley and LaVerda Mooneyham

9
Champion of Underfed Millions

WORLD VISION'S
STANLEY MOONEYHAM

"Tears are the vocabulary of the anguished soul. The poor cry a lot. To the poor, the destitute, and the refugee, day after day life is a grinding monotony of waiting for nothing. There is something excruciatingly sad about despair that knows no hope."

These and other profoundly moving observations have been expressed by Dr. Stanley Mooneyham in his important book *What Do You Say to a Hungry World?*

Stan Mooneyham thought he knew what privation was, but then God placed him in the work of World Vision International and he was in a face-to-face confrontation with poverty, hunger, starvation, and suffering such as he had never seen before. "The effect on my life then and later is incalculable," the distinguished-looking Mooneyham explains. "My conclusion is that poverty is like a bleeding wound that never heals, hemorrhaging strength and life out of the body and contributing to the chronic sickness of society. Poverty is the knockout punch in an uneven encounter. Someone has said that food is a celebration. I am just sad that so few have been invited to the party."

A number of years ago at a writer's conference in Minneapolis, Dr. Mooneyham, in talking to me about the influence of contemporary women on Christianity, remarked that his own wife played a tremendous role in influencing his life and his way of thinking. "LaVerda came to visit me in the hospital in Shawnee, Oklahoma. I was, of course, tremendously impressed with this very pretty sixteen-year-old who came with other members of the youth group in the church to visit me. She unhesitatingly expressed her convictions, and I knew that she wasn't about to date someone who wasn't out and out for Christ."

That "very pretty sixteen-year-old" was, in God's timing, to become the wife of this man destined to be in the forefront of those going in Jesus' name "to the scenes of disaster and hardship . . . the scenes of flood, typhoon, earthquake, famine and war."

LaVerda Mooneyham explains her first impressions of the then twenty-year-old Stanley Mooneyham. "From our first meeting I sensed that he longed to live life to the fullest and had a healthy attitude toward not only getting the best from life, but wanted to be a part of the action to accomplish for good. Stan graduated from Harrah, Oklahoma, high school at sixteen and joined the navy at seventeen. He served almost three years in the Pacific and saw battle."

When he came back to Oklahoma he was involved in a car accident. It was this accident that brought LaVerda to his bedside.

Upon his release from the hospital, Stan came to church worship services and began attending some of the youth activities. It was at this time he experienced his conversion to Christ. At a lakeside wiener roast, they had their first date.

"Stan's interest in the things of the Lord and his dedication grew rapidly," his wife says. "He felt definitely that God wanted his service and that he should accept this as God's will for his life and plan for the ministry." He was a naturally gifted writer and had planned to be a journalist. After his conversion his concentration was more on the study of the Bible, but through his college years he continued with journalism as a major.

"Stan has always been an extremely active person," his wife says, "never satisfied with just one job if he could accomplish two at once. While a college freshman he read something from Aristotle which seemed to fit his activist personality, so he adopted it as his life's motto: 'Where there are things to be done, the end is not to survey and recognize those various things, but rather to do them . . .'"

Stan laughingly recalls, "I'm sure some people would raise an eyebrow at a Christian having an Aristotelian saying for his life's motto, but I wasn't far enough into the Christian life at the time to know about such things as life verses that some people choose for themselves. Anyhow, this particular bit of wisdom from the ancient Greek philosopher has its biblical counterpart. Jesus said, 'I must work the works of him that sent me while it is day, for the night cometh when no man can work.'

"As LaVerda says, Aristotle's profoundly simple observation seemed to fit my personality, so I typed it out and taped it in the front of the Bible I owned after becoming a Christian. It's still there. Somehow, I don't think Jesus minds."

LaVerda carries on the story: "Attracted by many interests, Stan seemed to find his greatest joy in preaching. Earlier he had turned down an offer to serve as sports editor on the *Shawnee News-Star*, where he was a part-time reporter and feature writer, in order to give himself to preaching. In the summers between college years he expanded this part of his ministry by conducting evangelistic campaigns and youth conferences.

"Among the variety of things he still does, I think preaching is his first love.

"Stan's work through those early years changed many times, but with each new job he seemed to be learning or developing new talents. He tackled everything with zest and enthusiasm. With each opportunity he was always content to do that job to the fullest with no desire to climb the prover- bial ladder. Looking back, we can see that with every change God was leading into a new adventure and learning ex- perience. It seems as if his work has been a series of widening circles expanding to the worldwide service it has now become."

Of his childhood, Stan recalls: "Growing up as the son of a Mississippi sharecropper during the Depression, I knew privation and temporary hunger, but I never knew total despair." The youngest of seven childern, he was born on a farm in Mississippi and lived there with his parents until his family moved to Oklahoma when he was thirteen years old. His mother was a devout Christian, always praying for her family. She was an evangelist in the Church of God. His father was a Methodist and active in the community of "old harp" sings.

LaVerda tells of their marriage and the early years. "At the end of summer, just three months after our first meeting, many very important decisions were made which were to af- fect our future. Stan decided on a course of study and started to Oklahoma Baptist University. He began to prepare for the ministry and spoke whenever an opportunity arose. When he asked me to become his wife I gladly accepted, asking only that God's will be done in our lives but being totally unaware of what the future had in store.

"Most of the ministers' wives that I knew helped in some way in the small churches which their husbands pastored. Since I had studied piano and sung in small groups, I thought I could become the average friendly, helpful, encouraging pastor's wife and with a little study could teach Sunday School and take care of other duties like those.

"How wise is our God who only reveals a little of His will to us at one time. I'm sure I would have quit before getting started if I had realized that we would be living in two foreign countries and five different states with our four children, and that my husband's work would develop into a worldwide humanitarian effort."

A man's character does not emerge overnight. Stanley Mooneyham's did not. What were some of the building blocks that the Lord used to shape this man into the instrument he could use facing the crises of flood, famine, earthquake, and war in the far-flung corners of the world?

"Learning by experience has been a way of life for us," Mrs. Mooneyham shares. "The many experiences of those early years have been an asset down through the years. Stan has always learned by doing as well as studying."

Consider the doing—working his way through college as news writer on a city newspaper, pastoring a small church while still in college, commuting 120 miles daily his last year in college so that he could be a pastor and yet finish his education, always carrying a full study load, editing the college weekly newspaper. Those were the days of a meager salary and some support from the G.I. Bill. "But always our needs were met," LaVerda hastens to add.

A pastorate in Sulphur, Oklahoma, consumed their energies and time for the first four years after college graduation. Then Stan was offered the position of executive secretary for their denomination. "This was an opportunity to develop a new program, to found and edit the denominational magazine—it was all an exciting challenge for a twenty-seven-year-old. After much prayer and thought we decided that God must be leading in this direction. It meant a move to Nashville, Tennessee."

Stan began to travel throughout the United States in his new work, preaching and promoting in his role of administrator and editing the magazine. This gave him opportunity to meet many church leaders both in and outside of their denomination. It was all instrumental in broadening his interests and scope of vision.

"In 1957 he traveled to Europe preaching in Holland and Spain. It was the first of his numerous overseas trips," his wife says today.

In the next few years thing began to grow rapidly for the Mooneyhams—including their family. They had one daughter, Gwen, when they moved to Nashville. In three years' time they had outgrown their little house with the addition of two more babies, and now another move was in the offing.

"We moved to Illinois where Stan accepted a position with NAE (National Association of Evangelicals), first becoming the editor of *Action* magazine and later the director of information and field services of that organization.

"During his work there an ever-widening scope of Christian service and association with dedicated workers continued, with more travel to other countries. All of this was equipping Stan to analyze needs and situations. Stan always spoke up for what he believed in. He was able to advise and suggest better methods of evangelism in many instances."

The years in Illinois brought another addition to the Mooneyham family in the form of son Mark. Stan also developed a heart condition, which was to cause him problems in the years ahead. "After five years in Wheaton, in 1963 an unexpected invitation came from Billy Graham to attend his team retreat in Florida. Dr. Graham had met Stan only once," LaVerda relates, "but knew something of his work."

The end result of Stan's attendance at that retreat was acceptance of a position with the Graham Association. "It meant moving to Atlanta, Georgia, where the new offices for the traveling team were being located. We enjoyed living there for two years. Seemingly it was not meant for us to have roots. Stan was asked to be coordinating director of the World Congress on Evangelism. We were soon packed and off as a family to Berlin."

More learning experiences were in store for the

Mooneyhams. "It was Stan's first attempt at working on a long-term basis with Germans or other foreign nationals."

The congress held at Berlin's Kongresshalle in October 1966 was a colorful array of faces from many countries. "Our hearts were filled with joy and emotion when long lines of people in their variegated national dress paraded down one of Berlin's main streets. When that glad day arrived, our children were filled with awe and pride in seeing some of the results of their father's work and God's leading throughout that long year of preparation. The congress was of much help and encouragement in bringing better cooperation and ideas to those who attended."

After the congress, the Mooneyhams went to the small Spanish island of Majorca with their friends, Dr. and Mrs. Carl Henry, to work on the book *One Race, One Gospel, One Task.* "It was also a time of rest. Stan had worked hard and had not felt well for two or three months," Mrs. Mooneyham explains.

When they returned to Berlin, they made plans to close the office and their house and be ready to return to Atlanta at the end of January. "The first of December was the time for the annual Billy Graham Evangelistic Association Team meeting in Florida. Stan left Berlin to attend, never guessing that he would not be returning.

"One day the next week my telephone rang and the operator said there was a call from USA. Expecting to hear Stan's voice, I was surprised to hear 'This is Billy Graham.' He was calling to tell me that Stan was in the hospital with what they thought at the time was a coronary thrombosis. The next few days were filled with prayer. Many decisions had to be made.

"I decided to leave Berlin immediately with the children. Stan called during this time, his weakened voice barely above a whisper. He wanted to assure us he would be all right and told us not to rush to move back.

"Many friends were praying for him, and I could feel the strength of their prayers. Nevertheless, I wanted to be there, so the children and I left Berlin."

Later, after Stan's recuperation period in Florida, the Mooneyhams moved back into their Atlanta home. "We didn't realize it would be such a short stay," she says. "Just one year later we stored our furniture and were on our way to Singapore, where Stan was to be coordinator for the Asian Congress on Evangelism."

The family flew to Oklahoma to spend the Christmas holidays with members of their family enroute to Singapore. Before leaving the country, however, the Mooneyhams came to Texas to Houston's Methodist Hospital, famous for the heart surgery and transplants of Dr. Debakey. "After examination, Stan was told he needed surgery for removal of the pericardium in the heart area, which was restricting his heart from functioning properly.

"The operation was performed successfully, but it delayed our getting to Singapore for several weeks."

There followed more recuperative time on a ranch in Texas; then on to Honolulu, where Stanley Mooneyham took sick again. Certainly these were testing days; but God had his hand on the life of this dedicated man and his family.

"Finally Stan was able to travel and we were off to Singapore, the city inhabited by Chinese, Malaysian, Indians, British, Americans, and various other nationalities. Needless to say, living in Asia almost on the equator was a new experience. After the initial adjustment, we loved being there."

In retrospect, one can see the guiding hand of the Lord in these many moves. Planning this congress meant making new friends and contacts throughout Asia. All of this was to play a significant role in Mooneyham's later involvement with World Vision International, which serves so magnificently as a switchboard between people's concern and world need. His wife explains: "Since his experiences of work internationally, Stan has been serving on planning boards and committees which have been responsible for important decision-making in Christian leadership."

Life in Singapore brought some never-to-be-forgotten experiences to the Mooneyhams. "After the congress, a continuing office for promotion of Asian evangelism was set up there. We stayed until the school year was finished, returning in June, 1969. Stan had experienced a feeling of not knowing which way to turn in his work after the congress. This was of the Lord, because right at this time he was approached about the possibility of becoming president of World Vision International."

When the Mooneyham family returned, it was to settle in Arcadia, California, near the offices of World Vision in Monrovia. It was quite a change for them—the fast-paced California style of living, their oldest daughter off to college, two junior-highers, and a son in second-grade. But the Mooneyham family had learned much along the way about adapting to new situations and new life-styles.

Because of bad health, Dr. Bob Pierce had resigned two years previous to the arrival of Dr. Stanley Mooneyham as World Vision's president. Mooneyham brought to the organization a deep personal commitment that matched the emphasis of World Vision: a people-to-people involvement program bringing Christ and Christian social action as they minister to the whole man—body and soul—in every part of the world. This commitment to ease the pressing needs of other human beings finds Mooneyham traveling around the globe ministering to millions. There is a network of experienced field personnel who know their countries and who work side by side with the World Vision field directors.

Figures and statistics by no means tell the whole story, and such figures are constantly changing. But as an international vehicle for world evangelism and humanitarian efforts, in 1976 the organization was supporting more than one hundred thousand needy children in thirty-seven countries through the Childcare Program. They deliver tons of emergency supplies to people in desperate need—medical aid, food, clothing, emergency housing. There are imaginative self-help projects that are funded by the organization—farming efforts, water wells, showing the people how to read and write. They set up new Christian churches and encourage and help the national Christian leaders. Tens of thousands of people have found Christ through their evangelistic efforts.

In creative compassionate efforts, World Vision International, under the loving leadership of Mooneyham, has led the way in responding to the challenge of Christ who said, "I was hungry and you gave me food, I was thirsty and you gave me drink, I was a stranger and you welcomed me, I was naked and you clothed me, I was sick and you visited me, I was in prison and you came to me" (Matt. 25:35–36).

Dr. Mooneyham's wife, who is as close to the work as anyone and who knows how personally involved her husband is with the life and death struggle of the countless millions of needy people around the world, says, "There are a few experiences during the years since 1969 which stand out above the others. One was the beginning of World Vision's work in Cambodia in 1971 and the end of that same work in the spring of 1975, just a few days before the fall of Cambodia to the Communists."

In June 1970, when the war in Vietnam spilled over into neighboring Cambodia, the world watched, it seemed, uncaring. The people were unprepared both militarily and psychologically for this brutal assault on their land and their life. They were fighting with empty hands.

There were no medicines, no doctors. Death and destruction were everywhere.

Then World Vision came upon the scene. They provided the first truckload of relief supplies to reach Phnom Penh on the dangerous road from Saigon. Riding on that truck himself was none other than Stan Mooneyham.

"Why?" asked government officials. Stan tirelessly explained, "We are Christians. We've come here in the name of Jesus Christ to share his love with you and to help you in whatever way we can."

But that was just the beginning. Within weeks, additional relief supplies were on their way. Christians throughout the world began to respond as Mooneyham got the message out. People became involved in the pain of Cambodia.

The Khmer government responded favorably to these demonstrations of love and concern. Permission was granted to Mooneyham and World Vision to conduct evangelistic campaigns in the capital. This was a first in the history of the nation—a 99.9 percent Buddhist country. Response to the Christian message astounded Mooneyham and those who had come to share the Gospel message. Most of the people had never heard the name of Jesus before. The refugees approached the Cambodian church leaders and the World Vision people. "When we were most desperate you came and helped us. Now, sir, we would like to follow Jesus. Is it possible for us to have a church in our village?"

Not only was a small church established in that village, but substantial emergency relief, medical help, and refugee housing was provided throughout the country. A $400,000 hospital was constructed in Phnom Penh.

World Vision had operated for twelve years in Vietnam and five in Cambodia when the end finally came. "I felt as if a close relative had a terminal illness and I had to be as close to the death bed as possible, even though I knew it was terminal," Mooneyham related when telling how he supervised World Vision's chaotic evacuation from the country in April, 1975.

But LaVerda Mooneyham describes those events from a wife and mother's point of view. "On April 3, 1975, Stan and our son Eric, a second-year student in college, left for Cambodia and Vietnam. Eric used his spring vacation break to become photographer for this exciting but dangerous trip into these two countries just before their fall. A plane and pilot was chartered in Bangkok and tons of food and supplies were flown into Cambodia when all ground transportation was blocked.

"Many people were near starvation as the refugees from the countryside had come into the city of Phnom Penh. World Vision had relief centers and had built a hospital which was to be dedicated and opened the very week that the supplies were taken in. Twenty-three children who had been abandoned to World Vision's clinic and nutrition center under the care of Dr. Penelope Key were brought out to Bangkok and then on to the United States. The staff, too, was brought out at the last minute.

"Three days after Stan and Eric's trip into Cambodia the country was taken over, and the work there ended as far as we know. World Vision's assistant director, a young Cambodian, chose to stay but sent his wife and children out on the last plane.

"Knowing of Stan's great love for these people, I knew he might take risks if necessary to be of help to them. I nervously watched all the newscasts as the situation worsened daily. With husband and son and other World Vision friends of ours on the staff in such danger, I came to realize how utterly dependent we must be on God's leading.

"After two trips into Cambodia they flew into Vietnam taking food and supplies in under the risk of being hit by rockets there also."

Sarah Webb Barrell, correspondent for a New York newspaper, wrote of Operation Babylift, explaining the dangers and the drama surrounding those hours. "The trip took two hours," she reported, "and Phnom Penh finally came into view. We were given short, succinct instructions on what to do when we touched down: Forget about our belongings and sprint for the bunkers.

" 'They'll be firing when we land,' the pilot said, referring to Communist gunners surrounding Pochentong Airport.

"As if to echo his words a cloud of black smoke rose from the runway, where a fuel dump had been hit by an enemy rocket.

"Our plane touched down and rolled to a stop. . . .

"Three cars were waiting behind the safety of sandbags at one side of the airport. They carried the 23 orphans in straw baskets. Big, frightened eyes peered out from between the wicker strands. Two four-year old boys clutched string bags containing their belongings.

"Mooneyham and his crew, wearing flak jackets and helmets, unloaded relief supplies for Phnom Penh, and the children, still in their straw baskets, were placed aboard the plane.

"It taxied down the runway, lifted off and 23 lucky Cambodian children were bound for a new life on American soil."

Reflecting on that risky adventure, Stan Mooneyham says candidly: "I'm not really the hero type. There just come times in a man's life when he must do what he must do. I could not abandon the church and my Christian friends in Cambodia without a demonstration of love that identified with them in their agony. After all, most of them couldn't leave, and many of them wouldn't leave when they could. I had to somehow identify with that kind of commitment and courage."

He also talks about what his wife means to him in times like this.

"LaVerda is a special kind of person. She has to be. I often feel that the demands of my work are much harder on her than they are on me. Most of the time I am on the move, and during those six to eight months each year when I am away she must assume the waiting role. We both know that the Bible teaches that those who stay by have the same reward as those who are engaged in the battle, but I believe that waiting is still more difficult than going.

"Then there falls on her the added family responsibility. I can honestly say she has assumed this uncomplainingly and without developing a martyr complex. She has built the family life around my frequent and long absences and then shifted it back again when I come home. I know this requires an incredible degree of patience, self-sacrifice and love. And what a magnificient job she has done with our four beautiful children!

"Perhaps amazingly, there has never been any tension between us over those times when I feel it is necessary to be away. Never once has she said, 'Don't go,' although I am sure many times she wanted to say it. Even when we both knew there would be dangers, she has carried her fears quietly inside her heart. Her quiet faith and steady support have contributed more to what we have been able to do for Christ than can ever be measured this side of the judgment seat of Christ. If there are degrees of rewards in heaven, I gladly acknowledge that LaVerda's will be greater than mine."

Her support for the relief and evacuation efforts by her husband during the last days before Cambodia and South Vietnam fell was undergirded by her own knowledge of the situation there and her earlier participation in the ministries of Dr. Mooneyham in those countries. She had been with him during the last crusade in Phnom Penh and had thrilled inside as day after day she watched about half the audience respond to the invitation to receive Christ. She knew personally many of the people in both countries.

"Because of his special love for the Cambodians and Vietnamese, the loss of those two countries to the ministries of World Vision was a terribly depressing blow to Stan. When he and Eric returned, Stan was not only physically exhausted, but I could also see that he was emotionally wounded. It was several months before the depression left him and his emotions were healed, and during that time I could only stand by and pray for him. Where he hurt was deeper than I could reach and only the Holy Spirit could minister to him.

"Our comfort now," she says, "is in knowing that we did what we could while we could."

But Cambodia was only one place where the impact of World Vision's concern and love has been felt.

The World Vision TV specials are deeply moving presentations meant to touch the hearts of others so that they, too, will join in these efforts to bring help and hope to the world's suffering millions. "Stan traveled to Africa, India, Vietnam, Cambodia, and South America, along with Art Linkletter for filming that was used in *Children of Zero* and *Search for Survival*," his wife explains.

"Then he covered eighteen countries in eight weeks, gathering material for the book *What Do You Say to a Hungry World?* and filming on-the-spot footage for the five-hour telethon on world hunger that has raised millions of dollars for World Vision-assisted projects. The latest prime time television special was 'One to One,' a delightful musical production with Julie Andrews and the World Vision Korean Children's Choir.

"All the television programs are primarily appeals for help for the hundreds of projects that World Vision funds in the underdeveloped nations and disaster areas."

A new weekly television series, now in production with Stan Mooneyham as host and narrator, will be different, however. It will be a contemporary missions program, he says, showing the many exciting ways God is working in the world today. "Come Walk the World" will feature stories of the Holy Spirit's activities worldwide, interviews with Christian leaders from every continent, and stories about many modern-day heroes and heroines of the cross who are serving Christ in the out-of-the-way places as well as some of the world-s great cities.

When interviewed by the press, Mooneyham speaks with authority. "All of the political and military problems in the world today have no human solutions.

"They really don't. We are up against a brick wall humanly speaking. I don't have any human hope for this world but I know that God is in control."

In his book *What Do You Say to a Hungry World?* Dr. Stanley Mooneyham paints a picture of the situation worldwide that cannot be ignored; and then he asks questions that are on the minds and hearts of many and gives answers as guideposts to understanding. These are hard questions and harder answers, he says, but there are things the average person can do. (The reader is advised to read Dr. Mooneyham's book.) "The fact that the problems are complex does not mean they are insoluble. The problem is not technology or knowledge, but willingness to act.

"The words of Jesus in Matthew 24:31–46 contain a very disturbing thought. It is this: Jesus Christ is starving. It is impossible to avoid any other conclusion when you hear him say, 'I was hungry and you fed me. . . . When you did it to these my brothers you were doing it to me!' To feed the hungry is to render a personal service to Christ himself.

"As followers of Jesus, most of us enjoy gobbling up the goodies—fellowship with other Christians, air-conditioned places of worship, graded church school materials, potlucks, activities at the church. They are the fringe benefits of faith.

"What about the rest of the Gospel?" Stanley Mooneyham asks. "That part that talks about the importance of sharing in our Lord's suffering? Is that also an important part of our theology? How much have we felt the pain that God feels when a little skin-and-bones boy in Bangladesh dies from a simple disease just because his body had no more resistance? Are our hearts moved like the Master's when we see streams of refugees fleeing from their homes in Vietnam, running into social cesspools in inhospitable, overcrowded cities that offer neither security nor food?

"Do we, can we, feel the hurt? Are we really convinced that to care for others in their physical affliction is an indispensable part of the Christian life?

"We'd better believe it, because without it, we have only half a Gospel."

There was one other person who shed additional insight into the life and character of this remarkable man; it was his secretary, Nancy Moyer. Nancy said, "His compassion for people is true and there is virtually no limit to his willingness to be a stepping stone towards a better life for the people in our world who are hurting so badly. You're right—he's a marvelous man, and there's none that I know who is more unique or admirable."

"What about the rest of the Gospel?" Mooneyham asks. And it is the question I would like to leave with the reader as you consider what God would have you do.

Jim Reid

10
A Ministry of Presence

LAS VEGAS STRIP MINISTER
JIM REID

Casinos big as football fields, barges afloat on vast indoor ponds, acrobats and elephants traipsing through the lounges, an eight-hundred-dollar-a-night suite, a fountain as long as most city blocks, the world's largest chandelier—all this and more can be found in Las Vegas, Nevada. Some call it "Dream City," others "Fun City," and still others label Las Vegas as "Sin City." But there is one man who calls the city home, and who, in the late 1960s looked at the city and its glittering Strip and felt growing indignation.

To himself Jim Reid thought, "Why isn't someone trying to minister to these people?" The realization struck him that on a good night there may be as many as fifty thousand people populating the three miles of asphalt, neon, and lights forming the make-believe world called the Strip.

Jim Reid was pastor of a sixteen-member church in Henderson, a bedroom suburb fourteen miles southeast of Las Vegas, when such thoughts started colliding uncomfortably. He and his wife and children had lived in the entertainment capital of the world for four years, and in all that time had gone to see only one show on the Las Vegas Strip. On the occasion of his wife's birthday, however, some friends invited them to see the dinner show at Caesar's Palace. Jim Reid's attention was not focused on the stage, but rather, in his words, "on the people doing the acting."

"A little boy of eight or nine performed in the opening scene; being a preacher, I couldn't help wondering where he would go to Sunday school the next day. But I remembered he also had to do a second show that wouldn't be over until 2 A.M. So he probably wouldn't go anywhere to Sunday school or church."

The thought made him uneasy. Uncomfortable. "Besides the people in the show, there are stagehands and wardrobe people, waiters, busboys, and captains." His eyes roamed around the showroom. "Out in the casino there are dealers, cocktail waitresses, bartenders, keno runners, and a host of others who work these unusual shifts." And then it struck him, a still small voice at first, but one that grew stronger and louder in the days that followed: "This is a great mission field."

That night, while the show went on, Jim Reid's thoughts continued to collide. "Why don't you do something about this mission field? But God, property on the Strip and a building would cost a fortune. Don't you know I own the cattle on a thousand hills? If I'm in it, nothing is impossible." Jim envisioned it all—a split-level building with worship services held at unusual hours convenient to the show people.

The vision was shared by Jim with his wife, Janice, and for six weeks he nurtured the dream. He spent days cruising up and down the Strip looking for possible sites, and writing letters about property. But the doors all seemed closed. "I was suffering from an 'edifice complex,' " he jokes. "I could see no ministry without a building."

He tried, without success, to dismiss the idea of a Strip ministry from his mind as he continued with his church ministry in Henderson, Nevada. "I felt an uneasiness unlike anything I had ever felt before. In performing my regular pastoral duties I could not escape a recurring confrontation with the Strip." By night the city of Las Vegas shimmered in the distance on the valley floor; even in the daytime it was an imposing sight from the Henderson home and the side of the mountain on which the church stood.

Daylight or dark, the city of Las Vegas could not be ignored. "If Jesus lived here, would he be ministering to a handful of the faithful on this hill, or would he be out there with the thousands who need his redemptive message? It occurred to me that I was ministering to the one found sheep while the ninety-nine wandered lost in a maze of neon."

He sensed that God was telling him his ministry at the church had come to an end. "Lord, I can't resign the church. It's our only source of income. How could we live and pay the bills? Besides, what would I use for a building?"

It was at a mission colloquium in Mill Valley, California, some months later that Jim Reid received his answer. "I perceived the Lord saying to me, 'Trust me.'"

On his return home, Jim shared with his wife the decision. "If you are sure it's God's will," she said, "I'm with you." The Strip sparkled in the sun as Jim Reid and his wife sat in a parking lot where Flamingo Road meets the Strip and together they bowed their heads and thanked God for making his will known and for giving them this place to serve. "We dedicated the Strip and all the people on it to him." The next night he resigned from his church, thus launching the Koinonia ministry.

"Lord, there are no how-to books on this kind of ministry. How do I begin?" With the help of four interested friends and his family, Jim began. They incorporated as a church under Nevada law; they elected officers; they discussed possible plans. "We dropped the idea of renting even office space because of the cost. I then began to envision the ministry to be in the hotels and showrooms and not in an office. I knew I had to be available, so I had an answering service and a beeper and wore a one-way radio on my belt."

Jim and his Koinonia family knew that if a business is to succeed, it has to advertise. They lettered his Volkswagen on both doors, "Jim Reid, Chaplain to the Las Vegas Strip," with the beeper phone number. "I knew I wouldn't be permitted to distribute tracts in hotels and casinos, but no one would object if I had a calling card. So we had a variation of the Four Spiritual Laws of Campus Crusade printed." Now he was ready.

"Okay, God, here I am," Jim was praying as he waited for a stoplight at the corner of Tropicana and the Strip. "Now what do I do?"

He had prayed for help and the leading of the Holy Spirit. Now he felt an urge to go to the Flamingo Hotel. He walked through the door and faced the bellmen. "Hi! I'm Jim Reid, your friendly Strip chaplain." The first time he said it, he thought he'd choke on the words. "I'm here to minister to the spiritual needs of employees and guests of the hotel," he continued somewhat nervously. "Guess you have a lot of people around here who are uptight," it was half question, half comment. "I can always be reached," and he pointed to his beeper.

One of the bellmen looked at him and said, "Do you help bellmen too?"

"Sure," Jim replied. "Got time for a cup of coffee?"

"Yeah," the bellman responded, "let's go."

His name was George. "Maybe you won't want to waste any time on me," he ventured. "You see, I've been here eight years. I procure prostitutes for my guests," he hesitated waiting to see the impact this might make on "the friendly Strip chaplain."

There was no comment from Jim Reid.

"I sleep with prostitutes myself." Again he waited. "Are you sure you still want to talk to me?" George asked.

Jim assured him he did. Then George poured out his troubles: "I blow grass, use uppers and downers, even have some in my pocket right now. My wife's left me." There was more. In the days that fast turned into weeks Jim was to hear a repetition of George's story, with variations, of course, wherever he went.

The Stardust, the Dunes, Circus-Circus, back to the Flamingo, the Frontier Hotel—soon the balding, bushy-side-burned minister in his little VW became a familiar sight to the people who call Las Vegas home.

Roulette wheels spin and liquor flows twenty-four hours a day, but Jim Reid is right in the middle of it all every day. He can be found almost every night backstage, chatting with showgirls and stagehands. Or again, you might spot him on the casino floor, mixing with gamblers, pit bosses, and shills. Then, you may spy him in a phone booth, talking quietly with a prostitute or would-be-suicide.

"In a short time I met people addicted to alcohol, drugs, gambling, and sexual perversions," he quietly says. "One of the biggest problems in Las Vegas, as is to be expected, is habitual gambling. I cling to the belief that Jesus is the answer to any kind of addiction," Jim Reid affirms. "He can deliver anyone from anything that enslaves him, even self." Thus the Koinonia group, with Jim Reid as trailblazer, set out on their mission to help individuals bound by habits to break the yokes that held them enslaved.

Typical of those in the grip of such addiction was the organist at the Frontier Hotel. Under the strong urging of the Holy Spirit, Jim Reid made his way backstage one night. After announcing himself, the organist, without stopping his playing of the organ, said, "Man, that's weird, you being here."

"I'm sure God led me here," Jim replied.

"Man, is my life a mess. I was just sitting here playing this thing and wondering where I could go for help."

Jim Reid told him, "Bill, Jesus loves the hooked and can set them free. You can have a new life if you'll surrender yourself to Jesus and make him Lord." Bill was ready and desperate. Four months later he told Jim, "You know, Christ really can give you a new life."

Backstage Bible studies soon began to meet the needs of those searching for answers who were turning, as Jim Reid puts it, "to the whole metaphysical bag." Between shows Jim met with stagehands and discussed Edgar Cayce, reincarnation, psychic phenomena, and metaphysics. At the same time he talked to them about Jesus Christ and his power to change lives. Signs were posted announcing Bible study meetings between shows. "I now held Bible studies four nights a week, but still had no Sunday service," Jim explains. "But a preacher without a place to preach on Sunday is miserable."

One of the first converts from the Dunes Hotel Bible study was Randy, a stagehand at the hotel, who soon became Jim Reid's assistant. In time he was to lead Bible study groups himself, assist with prayer therapy and counseling.

It is not at all unusual for girls from the burlesque circuit to join the Bible studies. One such girl was Virginia, who earned $367 a week without clothes, but after becoming a Christian, Virginia chose to cover up and earn $260.

Jim Reid explains that once those to whom he preaches become Christians it's up to them whether they change their life-styles or occupations.

The first Sunday worship services were held in a most unlikely place for such a service—the Circus-Circus, a huge casino built in the shape of a circus tent. But then, actually everything about Jim Reid's work in Las Vegas has been and is unusual. "The services we held there were unforgettable," he explains. "On one wall of the room we used was a picture of a tattooed lady, on another a picture of a sword swallower entwined in a snake. We were ten feet from slot machines. The casino floor itself is covered with gaming tables and above the gambling area, circus acts perform. It was not unusual for Tony Steel, one of the performers, to dive sixty feet from the ceiling into a small dry sponge in the middle of a '21' pit, and to shortly after that join us in our worship service!

"The Circus-Circus has a midway with every conceivable carnival attraction. There are trapeze artists and ballet aerialists. The room we used for our worship services was originally designed for a girlie show, but it didn't seat enough people. It did accommodate enough people for our services however.

"In the middle of one of our services a woman stuck her head in the door and asked, 'What's going on here?' When she was told it was a church service, she responded with a huff, 'Well, I know God is everywhere, but this is ridiculous!' "

Ridiculous or not, the services continued there for four months with Pelousa the clown greeting people at the door and shaking their hands, and Tanya the elephant mingling with the onlookers. But the Oo-La-La Lounge was the beginning.

From there the services moved to the Gold Room of the Flamingo Hotel. The services are quite unlike usual church services—no announcements, no offerings. But always good music and a fifteen-minute message. Interruptions from the show personalities are not uncommon as they relate a personal problem and Jim Reid and his Koinonia family minister to needs.

Jim Reid explains the term Koinonia as being a New Testament concept of fellowship and communion. The idea is to form K-groups of individuals who want to get to know each other, who pray together and share in each other's personal spiritual struggles. It is the leaders of these groups who have helped Reid in follow-up on new believers, in counseling with them, and encouraging them to attend Bible studies and worship services. Along with this is the consistent emphasis, as they work with individuals, to instill in them the need to recognize the importance of daily Bible reading and prayer.

While the Las Vegas Strip is considered one of the most glamorous spots in the world, Jim Reid says, "Much of my ministry is anything but glamorous." Sometimes when the frustrations of the work get to him, Reid reminds himself of Jesus girding himself with a towel and washing the disciples' dirty feet. The work could rightly be called "the towel and basin ministry."

"After much prayer and thought I knew my priorities on the Strip would have to be, first, to serve people in Jesus' name whatever that involved, and second, to lead people to know Jesus as Savior when the opportunity arose. I related this to what Jesus said about giving a cup of cold water in his name."

The result of this decision was the formation of Yokefellow groups. This involves practical demonstrations of concern such as teaching English and reading to persons lacking basic education (of whom there are many on the Strip). "We spend many tedious hours with these people. Many of them can already read English when they come, but they do not have reading comprehension. I have used Creath Davis's book *Beyond This God Cannot Go* with great success. The first chapter speaks of the new birth. After they finish reading, we discuss what they've read. In discussing the new birth the conversation becomes less and less academic and more and more spiritual. It is the open door to invite them to surrender their life to Jesus and experience the new birth they have been reading about. Results have been amazing."

The dressing-room vernacular of the Strip people was also something Jim Reid had to become accustomed to.

Since the beginning of this ministry, Reid has enlisted the help of professional people—lawyers, doctors and dentists, for example—to whom he refers individuals who need specialized help and care. Then there is the benevolent fund—10 percent of the Koinonia income—which is dispensed to whoever needs help: plane and bus tickets for stranded tourists, meals for the hungry, clothes, gasoline, room rent, medical bills, medicine, and even on one occasion a complete set of false teeth. Hospital visitation is another part of the total ministry. A copy of *Good News for Modern Man* is always left on such hospital calls, and Jim Reid prays with patients. The results of such calls is far reaching.

Because the suicide rate in Las Vegas is seven times higher than the national average, Jim Reid finds himself working with the Suicide Prevention Center in Las Vegas. One woman whom he counseled opened up her purse and showed him enough Seconal and Nembutal to put half the Strip to sleep. "She'd been saving the pills for months," Reid explains, "and had carefully calculated the time, place, and manner of her death. In an effort to reach her I finally said, 'Betty, you've messed up your life so badly that the only answer for you is to kill yourself.' "

It had the desired effect. "This is exactly what she'd been planning, but hearing me say it made her recoil in shock." He was able to show her Galatians 2:20: "I have been crucified with Christ and I no longer live, but Christ lives in me."

The outcome of that confrontation was the realization that on her own she could not straighten out her life. Reid explained to her, "You must end it and let Christ take it over. He can give you a new life, a new beginning, if you will first die to self." She was willing to try God's way and uttered a beautiful prayer of repentance and surrender.

Pastoral counseling plays a major role in Reid's Strip ministry. Much of it is on a one-to-one basis in backstage encounters, as well as in homes and in the Koinonia office. The Yokefellow's prayer therapy forms an important part of the work.

Then there is always marriage counseling. "My goal is to preserve marriages if they can be saved," he emphasizes. "I have discovered that some marriages cannot be saved—but the individuals in those marriages can be. There are many marriages that have been saved, and there are many individuals whose lives have been salvaged."

The Strip ministry also has a twenty-four-hour hotline.

The number can be found in nearly twenty thousand of the hotel and motel rooms on the Strip. "But we aim to have our hotline number posted in every room in Las Vegas."

Jim Reid knows what it is to confront the devil. "I discovered that nearly 80 percent of the people to whom I was trying to minister were into some form of metaphysics. "Moreover," he underscores, "a high percentage are involved in witchcraft—casting spells and the whole business. Some on the Strip dabble in worship of Satan. Show people easily become involved in the occult, and there are those who are demon-possessed."

Jim Reid and those who work with him on the Strip have become an effective team in dealing with the demonic. "I am amazed how much the Bible speaks of the Christian warfare with demonic forces," he says, "as in Ephesians 6, for instance."

God's Word has struck home in other areas to Jim Reid in the Strip ministry. "I claim no gifts of healing," he says, "but there is a direct command to the elders of the church in James 5:14 and 15 to act on the request of anyone who is sick. I now act on the authority of God's Word, in obedient faith, and will annoint with oil and pray for healing. We have seen people become completely whole again," Reid affirms. "Scripture says God works in all things for good to those who are his. Oftentimes in the darkest days of an individual's illness we have seen the greatest spiritual growth."

The discoveries that Jim Reid and his Koinonia group have made in the years since the Strip ministry began have been joyful discoveries. "Many people think of Vegas as Sin City, a place where no one believes in or thinks about God," he says. "I confess that in my weaker moments I sometimes feel that way myself and, like Elijah, I'm inclined to say, 'I, only I, am left and Baal's prophets are 450. Poor me.'

"About that time God awakens me to the reality that he has his people even here who haven't bowed their knees to Baal. I'm thankful for these Christian brothers and sisters," he pauses, and adds, "There are many helping hands; many who have often lifted my spirits and reminded me that I am not alone in this battle."

At the outset of the Strip ministry Reid had no guarantee of an income. "I had determined not to solicit funds from any person or any hotel in Las Vegas. When I made my commitment to God about this ministry, I received assurance from God that I wouldn't have to go out and get money for my own support or for the work itself. And the money has come in. We have never asked for a special offering for anything, but whenever a need arose, God always met it. The few times we have been faced with a deficit, I did not panic. It's great not to have to worry about money. Our financial responsibilities have increased considerably as this ministry has grown, but God always meets our needs."

The employees on the Strip were Jim Reid's focus initially, but through the years his concern and work have broadened to include visitors to the city. "One conservative estimate said that 20 million people passed through Las Vegas in a recent year. I knew that if I could only reach 5 percent of these visitors, that a hundred thousand a year could be ministered to." The idea occurred to him that he should attempt to get New Testaments in modern English placed in the hotel and motel rooms.

As is his custom when confronted with a problem or a challenge, Jim Reid took the matter to the Lord in prayer. The answer came in the form of 47,000 copies of *Reach Out* (a special edition of *The Living Bible* New Testament) and 30,000 copies of *Good News for Las Vegas* (a special cover edition of *Good News for Modern Man*). "Placing the Bibles was the easy part of this project," he explains, "but preparation of each one was something else." Each one received a sticker on the cover telling each guest of the Koinonia ministry and its availability for counseling around the clock, and gives the office telephone number. The Bibles also were stamped on the inside and an insert stapled to the first page.

"We had a diverse group of people working to help us on our production line, young people from a local church, older folks (several different church denominations represented), dancers, showgirls, and stagehands. It was a striking example of what God's people can do working together when they have to."

But distributing Scripture to hotel and motel rooms was just one way to reach people with the gospel message. Reid successfully cracked the major communications medium in the city with his offer to write a weekly column in *Panorama,* the free tabloid that tells over 71,000 takers where to find almost anything in Vegas. "The response has been highly gratifying," he modestly acknowledges.

In addition to five Bible studies a week, there are six Yokefellow groups, and the Sunday evening worship services at the Flamingo Hotel. But Sunday morning worship services are also held at the Holiday Inn casino; and the service is broadcast on radio at prime time on Sunday mornings.

Jim Reid is an avid jogger, and some of his best ideas have come to him while jogging. "Some of these ideas are pretty far out," he confesses, "but many of the things we are now doing or planning to do on the Strip were first conceived during my jogging." His idea, for instance, of having a television program. The program is called "Good News," and the format includes Gospel music and interviews with Strip personalities who have had a personal encounter with Christ. When they are in town, well-known personalities such as Johnny Cash and singing groups like the Imperials and the Spurlows appear on the show.

"Doing the unusual in Jesus' name is exciting," he says, "but in this kind of ministry you are often misunderstood." Most of the flak he has received has come from preachers and other Christians. "Without exception," he says without hint of bitterness, "they just do not understand, and I have had to understand that they do not understand. I could have wasted a lot of time and energy by being defensive and fighting with my Christian brothers. Generally I refuse to answer the charges raised against me—I ignore the source and go about my work. I have adopted Nehemiah's philosophy. When the biblical Nehemiah was challenged by those who would have stopped his work, he simply said, 'I am doing a great work and I cannot come down. Why should the work stop while I leave it and come down to you?' " (Neh. 6:3).

As Jim Reid sees it, there are three prerequisites for anyone beginning an unusual type of ministry: First, he must know who God is. His relationship with Christ and his knowledge of the work of the Holy Spirit must be intimate, personal, firsthand, and unshakable. Second, a man must have an unshakable relationship with his wife. There must be, on her part, complete trust and understanding. The love relationship must be a secure, strong one. And third, a person attempting an unusual type of ministry must have a good, secure relationship with himself. There is, for instance, the threat of success and the spiritual pride that can accompany this. There is also the ever-present temptation to compromise one's self and the ministry. "Sexual overtures have been made to me," the friendly Strip chaplain says, "and I'm not even a Burt Reynolds type!"

In addition to these three requirements, Jim Reid has another philosophy which has enabled him to get in and get the job done. "I have had to learn to be flexible. When I first ventured out on the Strip I wore the conventional ministerial dark suit and narrow tie. I had a pious look. No wonder I had difficulty getting backstage at some of the hotels. My frustrations caught up with me," he concedes, "and I went to a men's clothing store and bought a body shirt, vinyl boots, and flared pants." This was more appropriate garb, he soon learned, for entree behind the scenes.

"Now I am well enough known and secure enough in my chaplaincy that I don't need to dress that way," he relates, "but if I hadn't been willing to do something different, I might still be writing letters to managers and receiving no answers." Flexibility.

The ability to develop a nonjudgmental attitude towards those he wanted to reach might be another definition for his role as Strip chaplain. "I also had to change my ideas concerning nudity. My thinking when I first went onto the Strip was that any girl who danced nude must surely be a prostitute, or at least a loose woman."

Once again, Jim Reid prayed, seeking help: "God, help me to see these girls as people for whom Jesus died and not just as bodies," was his prayer. "And that's what happened. Soon I was meeting with them and sharing the love of Jesus. I learned that many of these girls are wives, many of them mothers who do laundry and fight crabgrass and do all the other things women do. Only they work unusual hours and work nude.

"Flexibility was needed in my theology—not that I compromised any of the fundamentals of the faith. Flexibility has come to mean the ability to look myself in the face and admit I am wrong. That hasn't come easily for I am conditioned the same way many other preachers and Christians are.

"After I began the Strip ministry, I had to determine my approach. Arthur Blessitt has had a strong influence in my life, and the initial decision to get into this work. But I had to recognize that I wasn't Arthur Blessitt, and therefore his way of witnessing wouldn't necessarily be best for me. Some call my basic structure or approach the ministry of presence, and I think that aptly describes it."

Thus it was that Jim Reid decided on the friendly Strip chaplain approach, with a nonjudgmental attitude. "If I began by condemning people for drinking, gambling, dancing nude, or whatever, I would alienate them before I even knew their names. I remembered that Jesus condemned religious leaders for their hypocrisy, but he never condemned sinners for their sins. On the contrary, he said he came to save them from their sin and consequently was himself condemned for associating with 'tax collectors and sinners.'

"Later I gained a real insight into Jesus' ministry from one of my English class students, a Greek fellow. I learned that the Greek work *hamartolos* is always translated 'sinner' in the King James version of the Bible, but that it is the modern Greek word for 'prostitute.' I wondered whether it could have meant that in Jesus' time as well. Wow! I thought, Jesus would have been right at home on the Strip."

Seeking to follow Jesus' example, Reid, therefore, has developed the fine art of listening. "I always listen first," he explains. "Then I try to meet whatever material need may be present. The last thing I do—but I always do it—is to tell him about God's love for him in Jesus Christ. I then make an effort to lead an individual to a commitment of his or her life to Christ as Savior and Lord.

"My agreement with God at the outset of this ministry was that he would be God and I would be his messenger. My job, therefore, is to tell people about God's love for them in Jesus Christ and to demonstrate the new life available to them— but it is the Holy Spirit's job to produce the change in their lives. The Holy Spirit can do what the preacher cannot. I have discovered he is wholly trustworthy."

And so the work on the Las Vegas Strip goes on. The changes that are taking place are nothing short of miraculous. But then, that's what Christianity is all about. Ask Jim Reid, the friendly Strip Chaplain, and he'll point you to Jeremiah 32:27: "Behold, I am the Lord, the God of all flesh; is anything too hard for me?"

If you happen to be in Las Vegas and you see someone jogging—baldheaded, bushy sideburns, glasses—chances are it's Jim Reid, dreaming dreams, envisioning ways and means to reach people with the message that Christ is the only adequate answer to man's spiritual dilemma and need for fulfillment.

Dick and Wanda Ross

11
Mr. Media Man

MOVIE PRODUCER
DICK ROSS

We take for granted the superb Christian-oriented motion pictures and television programs that it has been our privilege to see (especially since the late 1940s), forgetting that back of these deeply moving films and TV spectaculars is the genius of gifted individuals who are using their creative abilities for the Lord. One such individual, highly respected in the communications industry, is Dick Ross, president of Production Associates, Inc., a Hollywood-based firm.

Producer-director Dick Ross began his cinema career following World War II and has remained in the forefront of motion picture and television evangelism. Recognized internationally as a leader in the development of production and distribution techniques, Ross has given unstintingly of himself year after year to raise the standards of creative and technical excellence in the proclamation of the Message. But where did it all begin? How does a man become so motivated?

For years I had been seeing the name Dick Ross flash across both the movie and television screen. It seemed that every time a new major motion picture with a Christian message came into being I saw the name of this man. I knew a little about him, linking him with such film all-time greats as *The Cross and the Switchblade, The Late Liz, Lucia, Oiltown USA, The Heart is a Rebel, Man in the 5th Dimension,* and others: but there was so much I did not know. Would Dick Ross consent to having his story be told? This tremendously admired and successful man, was he approachable? This gentleman who has so tenderly and skillfully told the life stories of so many others, what about his own story?

It was with a great amount of interest and excitement that we looked forward to our first meeting with Dick Ross and his charming wife, Wanda, in their Van Nuys, California, home. We soon discovered that Ross is not only a big man physically, but he has a heart that matches his stature. Later, he was to write and say of his wife: "Wanda's relationship to my work has always been that of a silent partner. Her interest is deep seated, but she has a low profile when it comes to involvement in the business, a characteristic I appreciate, having known too many husband and wife relationships to be weakened by too much meddling by the other partner." Wanda, that day, retreated quietly after our initial introduction. When we had finished our conversation she rejoined us—the gracious hostess, adding that beautiful perfect dimension that complemented the Dick Ross image.

Ross said, "Wanda's spiritual support is unmistakable. Without it, I couldn't operate at all. We've long since passed the point where we flippantly quote Bible verses to solve every problem. The baffling and the unexplainable in God's dealings with his children are too numerous to deny. I'll have a bundle of questions to ask when I get to heaven; of course, among them, how God in his mercy has been able to use me."

But use him, *he has!*

Ross tells his story like this:

"At noon on August 22, 1944, the B-24 Liberator bomber to which I was assigned as navigator began its bombing run on targets in the rich Upper Silesian oil fields of the Third Reich. I was sitting at my navigational desk on the flight deck of the aircraft where I could look forward between the shoulders of the pilot and copilot. The sky just ahead was black with a curtain of exploding antiaircraft shells. I heard Wendell Garret, the pilot, shout, 'We'll never get through that stuff!'

"As we penetrated the turbulent air of ack-ack I heard the bombardier's words on the intercom, 'Bombs away!' And a moment later the aircraft staggered from an obvious direct hit. The voices of the ten men aboard assured the pilot that no one had been injured by shell fragments, but almost immediately the smell of high octane gasoline filled the plane's interior. Looking back into the bomb bays I saw fuel pouring like rain through the still-open bomb bay doors. It was obvious our gas tanks had been riddled by flak.

"When the pilot shouted to his copilot to 'feather one!' I knew we'd lost an engine. The Liberator fell behind the formation, and we began a slow descent, unable to maintain altitude or speed. Hurriedly I studied the map on which I had been projecting our course, noting the danger areas of antiaircraft concentration, which were clearly marked at our morning intelligence briefing back at our headquarters near Foggia, Italy. Giving the pilot a course to follow that just possibly might enable us to reach Switzerland and relative safety from capture, I then began to explain our position to the rest of the crew, advising them how to make their way to the Swiss border if we had to bail out and were separated.

"In minutes we were alone in the sky, except for shell bursts from artillery along our agonizing route to the southwest. At 1,500 feet the pilot gave the order to bail out. I remember taking one last look forward and noting that Garret was standing up on one rudder pedal, trying to keep the bomber rightside up so we could have a chance to make a good jump. It seemed so incongruous to walk away from my navigational desk with its instruments and my prized chronometer. Drenched with gasoline I walked along the bomb bay catwalk, the wind buffeting my steps. There was a moment of hesitation. After all, no one practices with a parachute in heavy bombardment. I had never even taken the time to fit the harness properly to my body, for I never expected to use it.

"As my body arced away from the aircraft, I looked forward to see the doomed bomber in a shallow gliding turn. To the rear a string of my colleagues were hanging from their already opened parachutes. As I pulled the ring and felt the almost immediate jar of my chute opening, I had a spiritual experience that I shall never forget as long as I live. I look back through the years upon it as a turning point in my life. It was as if God's hand was suddenly extended in an embracing gesture of protection. Across my mind flashed an overwhelming assurance that this was not the end. My life would be spared for some special service, the nature of which was unknown to *me* then.

"Looking down I saw I was over a rural part of the Hungarian countryside. Farmers and field troopers were gathering, tracking my descent. I felt my body slip through the branches of a leafy tree, then a thudding jar as I hit the ground and rolled harmlessly in the dirt. Unsnapping my harness I stood to my feet and looked around at a complete circle of farmers with pitchforks, shovels, some guns—each face a study in hate. For Lieutenant Dick Ross of the 15th Air Force, the war was over.

"In the nightmare of capture, interrogation, and gathering of the rest of our crew in a local jail, God used a simple but meaningful article to spare my life. As I braced myself for a fearful beating by the farmers and field troops, one young man in the group suddenly noticed I was wearing a wedding ring. He pointed it out to the rest of the men, comparing it with a wedding band he also wore. Suddenly the pressure was off, and a softening of the group's attitude took place.

The young man took a position alongside me as we walked to the nearest village, as if to protect me from further danger.

"I have often thought of that dramatic incident during the years that followed, particularly Wanda's unwitting part in the preserving of a life and God-given talents that he was to graciously use in coming years.

"My career in communications had begun before World War II with broadcast experience during my student years at John Brown University. Winning an announcer's competition at the university's radio station, KUOA, I had had an opportunity to develop a style of performance, learned the rudiments of radio scriptwriting and studio production.

"An opportunity to advance my radio career prior to graduation took me to the Pacific Northwest, where I became program director of KMO, Tacoma, which was the key station of the northwest division of the old Don Lee-Mutual network. It was there that I met my wife, then a student at Simpson Bible Institute, which later became Simpson Bible College, in the San Francisco area. We were married in December of 1939, during the hectic Christmas season when a broadcaster's schedule is at its peak.

"The call of God to a life of discipleship had been evident years before when at the age of twelve I gave my heart to Christ at my mother's knee. But to actually serve him in other than a layman's service, it remained for a brief call from the Moody Bible Institute of Chicago to help get their broadcast activities onto a full-time schedule, to realize that there was something more than a layman's relationship in store. Four years with Irwin Moon at the new Moody Institute of Science followed the war, during which I was privileged to help create *God of Creation, God of the Atom* and *Voice of the Deep*. It was during those years that I recognized the power of the motion picture to motivate viewers.

"A year between the two Moody associations as night

supervisor of operations at the Don Lee-Mutual Network headquarters at KHJ, Los Angeles, enabled me to maintain my professional progress. In fact it was this tenure that enabled me to follow my association with Dr. Moon with a period of time at W6XAO, Channel 2 at that time, in Los Angeles. As the sole production employee of the station atop Mount Lee, overlooking Hollywood, I had a priceless opportunity of learning the art of live television at the time it was just beginning to flex its muscles, long before it became the most influential medium in global communications.

"In fact, it was while I was with the Don Lee television operation in 1949–50 that Dr. Bob Pierce was scheduled to run film of his recent trip to China. Our professional relationship became a deeply personal one, God giving him the task of challenging me to launch out on my own as a producer and director of motion pictures and television vehicles.

"It was also Bob Pierce who introduced me to Billy Graham during the evangelist's historic first Los Angeles Crusade. That encounter, following the production of a number of pictures for Bob's organization, World Vision, led to the merging of my company and Billy Graham Evangelistic Films, the combined operation becoming World Wide Pictures which I was privileged to head for fourteen exciting years.

"My first picture for Billy was *The Portland Story*, made as a documentary during his 1950 crusade in the City of Roses. It was the public reaction and support to that fledgling effort that gave all of us the encouragement to launch an ongoing program of both dramatic and documentary motion pictures that soon graduated from civic auditoriums and church sanctuaries to theaters and the daring decision to adopt a paid admission policy *(The Restless Ones)*.

"I guess the most ambitious undertaking until the current *The Late Liz* was the picture I made for the New York World's Fair, *Man in the 5th Dimension*. For two years it ran in a specially constructed pavillion on a giant screen in 70 millimeter. A follow-up program made use of an invitation at the close of the film to counsel those registering a decision to accept Christ as Savior.

"In 1965 God led me into a television emphasis out of which my present activities grew. Production Associates was formed and based on the NBC-Burbank lot, where I developed the Oral Roberts' contact specials: quarterly prime-time music-variety shows that mounted Oral with guest star celebrities, and that climaxed with a spiritual challenge in the language of the now. ARB ratings were incredible, numbering in excess of 30 million viewers on occasion. We also did the weekly Sunday half-hour series 'Oral Roberts Presents.'

"With Kathryn Kuhlman's death, I ended nearly ten years of association in the producing and directing of 'I Believe in Miracles.' Nearly five hundred shows, made at CBS Hollywood, presented music and interview materials in the context of God's healing power.

"Throughout the past twelve years, the spiritually oriented vehicles have been accompanied by just enough commercial activity to keep my hand in network television and to avoid my being typed solely as a religious producer. A Bob Hope Special for Mutual of Omaha, twenty-six comedy hours with George Jessel, ten 'Something Special' music-variety hours with such stars as Peggy Lee, Roger Williams, Buddy Greco, Jean Pierre Aumont, Frankie Avalon, and many more. And of course there have been the commercials, including the original Checkerboard Square device of the dog chasing the miniature covered wagon across the kitchen floor! These more crass commercial efforts have enabled me to establish contacts that have been put to good use in involving stars who have a spiritual rapport with such shows as the Oral Roberts and Morris Cerullo series. Pearl Bailey has become a close friend, for example, and I've watched her grow spiritually in a way that enables her to make a solid spiritual impact on the international scene.

"Between times, I have taken the time to produce and direct two motion pictures independently, *The Cross and the Switchblade* and *The Late Liz*, both of which are still in current release, and which have established the fact that there is a backbone of the American population that will support something meaningful at the box office, despite the disenchantment that the theatrical realm has created with its excessively permissive motion picture themes.

"The future? Well, as long as God gives me the strength and inspiration to create—and the economics to bring my creations to both the large and small screens of theatrical and television release—I am committed to do just that. When more people can be reached in sixty minutes or two hours than the Apostle Paul addressed in a lifetime of preaching, we must use the media as never before. We are seeing the decline of our culture and civilization just as surely as Gibbon reports it in the Roman Empire context. What we do, we must do quickly. God helping me, I want to be in the vanguard of those who are making an impact on the unchurched, the outsiders. Others can devote their time to the Christian millieu. My sympathies and concerns are with those who have never really been presented with anything but a caricature of Christ. Committing one's life to Christ as Savior and Lord is as natural as breathing. Offering that experience in an equally natural and credible way, through the medium of sight and sound, is my calling—and the reason, I am confident, that God allowed a Hungarian farmer to spare my life."

I could not help but wonder if the Hungarian farmer ever saw a Dick Ross produced and directed film and, if so, did he recall the young navigator's name and make an association.

But what of his wife Wanda, who played such a dramatic, albeit unwitting, part in sparing the life of Dick Ross? For her, after marriage there came a time of adjustment, with Dick's mother living with the young couple for most of ten years. "This was a difficult time for me," says Wanda, "for my life was never really my own. So I either had to grow up and mature in Christ, finding stability in him, or fall by the wayside. And, of course, all of this while trying to be a good wife and mother to two children."

By now a daughter, Sylvia, and a son, Rick, had been born to Dick and Wanda Ross. Dick's father had been concert-master of the San Francisco Symphony at the time of the great earthquake, but he died shortly after Dick's birth in 1918. This explains the close relationship between mother and son and the necessity for Dick's mother to be a part of Dick and Wanda's homelife for a number of years. Dick feels that his father's musicianship and composer's talents un-doubtedly contributed a great deal to his creative gifts and heritage.

Wanda continues her part of their story: "The years Dick spent in association with the Billy Graham organization found him away from home for weeks at a time. I had to learn total dependence on God. Only with God's help and grace did we manage to come out whole persons with a healthy marriage. I can only credit him with the fact that we have two wonderful children who have a healthy father im-age, both learning to cope with their own marriages and children.

"It gives me great joy to look back and see what God wrought out of confusion, heartache, and frustration—recalling times of real joy and happiness, discovering the order he has brought out of chaos. Without Christ in my life and a few faithful friends who prayed earnestly for me through the years, I'm certain I would not be what I am today. I like to think that the Lord through the years has formed me, at least partially, into a mature person in Christ, able to feel others' infirmities and heartaches because of my own experiences. How successful has been my yieldedness in allowing God to develop my life is for others to assess. But I do know that with Dick away so much of the time, I had to discover fulfillment in my own life. There had to be more than housework and care of children.

"Perhaps the crucible of those years is what prepared me for the deacon work in our nearby church. It has become one of my greatest joys. Through the years, the sick and the shut-ins have been a great part of my life, and I'm grateful to God for this fulfillment.

"I have had more than my share of happiness and the good things of life. But it has been the hard trials along the way that God has used to mold me and make me into Christ's image. Whatever I am, it is all by his grace."

Who better than one's husband is capable of assessing one's contribution and yieldedness to God? Of Wanda, Dick remarks: "Few people I have ever known have the gift God has given Wanda in ministering to the sick, the oppressed and distraught. God has raised up people like my wife to be his instruments in helping others to cope. It is one of the most sacrificial tasks of the Church, and usually is the least recognized and rewarded other than by those who actually are the beneficiaries of it."

Certainly God doesn't want us to waste any of our experiences—good or bad—and this Wanda Ross has recognized and done to her eternal credit.

Dick Ross was honored with a Doctor of Humanities degree from John Brown University in 1972. He is an elder in the Presbyterian Church of Sherman Oaks, California, where his wife is a deacon.

The name Production Associates is the hallmark of quality in spiritually oriented cinema and television. As a concerned citizen and a Christian viewer of such media, knowing what I now know about the man back of such productions I thank and praise the Lord for sparing the life of Dick Ross during World War II.